KB259975

Mr. Native 원서 읽기

QBQ!

The Question Behind the Question

John G. Miller 지음 | 정호섭 해설

한언

QBQ! THE QUESTION BEHIND THE QUESTION
(Bi-Lingual Edition)

펴   냄   2008년 4월 1일 1판 1쇄 박음 • 2008년 4월 5일 1판 1쇄 펴냄
지 은 이   존 G. 밀러
해   설   정호섭
펴 낸 이   김철종
펴 낸 곳   (주)한언
          등록번호 제1-128호 / 등록일자 1983. 9. 30
주   소   서울시 마포구 신수동 63-14 구 프라자 6층(우 121-854)
          TEL. 02-701-6616(대) / FAX. 02-701-4449
책임편집   윤혜영 hyyun@haneon.com
디 자 인   김하늘 hnkim@haneon.com
홈페이지   www.haneon.com
e-mail   haneon@haneon.com
          이 책의 무단전재 및 복제를 금합니다.
          잘못 만들어진 책은 구입하신 서점에서 바꾸어 드립니다.
I S B N   978-89-5596-475-2 03740

Mr. Native 원서 읽기

QBQ!

The Question Behind the Question

QBQ! THE QUESTION BEHIND THE QUESTION
(Bi-Lingual Edition)

I saw the angel in the marble and I chiseled until I set it free.

_Michelangelo

원서를 읽어야 하는 이유

영어 공부 잘하는 비결?

　직장인들에게 영어 공부는 평생 떠안고 가야 할 숙제다. 중학교부터 대학교까지 10년 넘게 영어를 해왔지만 듣기와 말하기는 커녕 읽기조차 쉽지 않다. 도대체 왜 읽기조차 정복되지 않는 걸까? 사람들은 읽다가 이해가 안 되어 막히면 읽기를 포기해버린다. 하지만 당신 혼자 그러는 것이 아니니 너무 의기소침해할 필요는 없다. 읽기는 누구에게나 어려우니까.

　그렇다면 어떻게 해야 할까? 개인마다 차이는 있겠지만 과연 얼마나 '영어를 즐기고 시간과 열정을 쏟았느냐' 에 달려있다. 여기에 구체적인 팁 몇 가지를 알려주겠다.

1. 자신의 수준에 맞는 글을 읽어라. 남들 읽는다고 해서 영자신문이나 두껍고 어려운 책을 읽을 필요가 없다.

2. 읽는 중간에 사전을 찾기 위해 멈추지 마라. 그러면 문맥의 흐름을 놓치게 되고 이해의 정도도 떨어지게 된다.

3. 단어 순서대로 읽어라. 우리말로 바꿔서 해석을 하려고 하는 순간 영어는 어려워진다. 그냥 영어 어순 그대로 읽고 이해해라.

4. 본인에게 필요한 정보, 재미있어 할 만한 글을 찾아라. 그러면 스스로 자연스럽게 동기부여가 될 것이다.

인내를 가지고 오랫동안 꾸준한 열정을 보여줄 때 영어를 읽는 눈, 듣는 귀, 말하는 입은 선물처럼 주어진다.

직장인들을 위한 안성맞춤형 주제와 난이도!

많은 사람들이 원서를 읽겠다고 마음먹고 책을 펼쳐들었다가도 모르는 단어나 해석하기 어려운 문장을 만나면 중간에 읽기를 포기하곤 한다. 영어 공부를 위해 원서를 고를 때는 주제와 난이도를 꼼꼼히 따져봐야 한다. 어휘의 난이도가 과연 나의 수준에 맞는지, 주제가 너무 딱딱하거나 혹은 유치하지 않은지 말이다. 이런 전제조건이 충족되지 않으면 한 문장 한 문장 읽어나가기가 힘겨워지고 학습효과는 기대할 수 없다.

이 책은 직장인 독자들이 관심을 가져야 할 자기계발이나 처세와 관련된 내용이다. 회사 업무 효율을 높이고 행복하게 일할 수 있도록 도와주는 재미있고 실용적인 내용이 펼쳐질 것이다. 그리고 막히는 부분이 없이 단숨에 읽을 수 있도록 오른쪽 페이지에는 원문을, 왼쪽 페이지에는 단어 설명과 문장 해설을 배치하였다. 이야기의 흐름이 끊기지 않도록 배려한 것이다. 또 중간 중간에 미국에서도 바로 써먹을 수 있는 회화 표현을 실었다. 마지막에는 한글 요약문을 실어 본문의 내용을 확인할 수 있도록 했다.

핑계와 변명, 불평 대신 당신의 가슴에 QBQ를 던져라!

우리는 불평을 하면 할수록 더욱 무능한 사람으로 보인다는 사실을 모른다. 우리가 스스로를 변명하고 방어하느라 급급한 사이에 우리의 경쟁자는 QBQ로 앞서 간다. 문제 이면에 숨어 있는 핵심을 꿰뚫는 질문, QBQ! 이 책은 우리가 무엇을 모르고 있는지, 지금 당장 무엇을 어떻게 해야 하는지, 어떻게 더욱 유능한 사람으로 거듭날 수 있는지 그 해답을 속 시원하게 가르쳐줄 것이다.

한국어판으로 출간되어 많은 국내 독자의 사랑을 받았던 《바보들은 항상 남의 탓만 한다》를 이제 원서로 만나볼 수 있다.

Acknowledgments

Many thanks to:

David Levin, my friend, coach, and writing partner. Without his vision, this book would never have happened.

Special thanks to my most important team—the one at home in Denver, Colorado, USA

The kids: Kristin, Tara, Michael, Molly, Charlene, Jazzy and Tasha, for putting up with Dad and his hectic schedule during this project.

My wife, Karen, for gently encouraging me to do this rewrite of my first book, Personal Accountability, and most of all for being my best friend.

Contents

billboard 광고 게시판 **towering** 우뚝 솟은 **loom** (사물이)크게 보이다
point the finger 손가락질하다 **carafe** 유리컵, 물병(여기서는 커피포트에 커피
를 받는 잔을 의미)

· · ·

What ever happened to personal responsibility? '당신의 책임감에 무슨
일이 있는 건가요' what happened to는 '~에 무슨 일이 있나요' '~은 어찌
된 건가요' 의 뜻으로 ever를 사용해 강조할 수 있다.
Jump out at me. '나에게로 튀어 들다' 즉, '내 눈에 확 들어왔다'
pardon me. '저기요?', '실례합니다' 라는 뜻으로 상대방의 주의를 요구할
때 사용한다. 보통은 상대방의 말을 못 알아 들었을 때 사용하는데 sorry?,
exc-use me?도 이와 같은 의미로 쓸 수 있다.

14

What Ever Happened To...

From a billboard towering over the Houston freeway loomed this question:

"What ever happened to personal responsibility?"

I don't know who put it up there, but it sure jumped out at me. For one thing, it seemed so clearly true. What has happened to personal responsibility? Why does it seem the only thing people know how to do any more is point the finger else where, blaming something or someone else for their problems, their actions, their feelings? Some examples:

I was looking for some coffee in a gas station convenience store but the carafe was empty, so I said to the person behind the counter, "Pardon me, there's no coffee in the pot." He pointed at a coworker not 15 feet away and

department 담당구역, 담당 **cross-country flight** 국내선(비행기) **intercom** 인터폰 **catering** 기내식 조달업체 **apparently** 분명히, 명백히 **carry-out**=takeout **pacing back and forth** 왔다 갔다 서성이다 **out of the blue** 불쑥, 느닷없이 **shift** 교대 **struck** strike의 과거분사

• • •

I felt strongly about it. '나는 강하게 그것에 동의하는 바이다'

said, "Coffee is her department!"

Department? In a roadside gas station the size of my living room?

Another: On a cross-country flight, the flight attendant got on the intercom and said, "Sorry, everyone, but the movie we promised you will not be shown today. Catering put the wrong one on board."

And this: The carryout pizza place had apparently lost our order, so I was pacing back and forth waiting for our pizzas while my hungry family waited in the car. Suddenly, out of the blue, the young man behind the counter said, "Hey, don't blame me, my shift just started!"

In one form or another, we often hear, "It's not my fault," "It's not my job" or "It's not my problem." The billboard jumped out at me partly because I agreed with it so much. But the other thing that struck me was that someone would feel strongly enough about personal responsibility to put it up on a billboard in the first place.

I felt strongly about it too, and that's why I wrote this book.

Who is this book for? Anyone who's ever heard questions like these:

"When is that department going to do its job?"

responsibility 어떤 특정문제에 대한 책임 **accountability** 자신의 행동과 그에 대한 설명의 책임 **go right to the heart** 본론으로 바로 들어가다 **conversely** 반대로, 꺼꾸로 말하면 **turn around** ~쪽으로 돌리다, 바꾸다 **refine** 정제하다, 연마하다 **resonate** 울려 퍼지다

• • •

Who dropped the ball? '누구에 실수일까?' 라는 뜻의 관용표현이다.

• • •

What happened to Judy? She never answers my call.
She's just been through a divorce.
주디에게 무슨 일 있나요? 전화를 안 받네요.
몰랐어요? 지금 이혼을 이겨내고 있어요.

"Why don't they communicate better?"

"Who dropped the ball?"

"Why do we have to go through all this change?"

"When is someone going to train me?"

These questions seem innocent enough, but they indicate a lack of personal responsibility—I actually prefer the term "personal accountability"—and go right to the heart of many of the problems we face today.

Conversely, turning our thinking around and asking more personally accountable questions is one of the most powerful and effective things we can do to improve our organizations and our lives.

The Question Behind the Question® (QBQ®) is a tool that's been developed and refined over the years that helps individuals—including me—practice personal accountability by asking better questions.

I've been writing and speaking about this concept since 1995, and the topic resonates as deeply today as it ever has. Nearly every day I hear new success stories of improved productivity, greater teamwork, reduced stress, healthier relationships and better customer service.

The benefit people enjoy the most about the QBQ, though, is a personal one: Once they start practicing QBQ

a lack of ~의 부족

• • •

If you're frustrated by what you see as a lack of responsibility in others. '만약 당신이 책임감 없는 다른 사람들로 인해 좌절했다면'

thinking, things just seem to go better. People have more fun. Life is simply more satisfying and enjoyable for those who choose the way of personal accountability.

So if you've heard questions like those listed earlier, if you're frustrated by what you see as a lack of responsibility in others—or if you recognize some of that thinking in yourself—this book is for you. Enjoy!

downtown 도심 **jammed** (사람들로) 꽉 찬 **grab** 급히 잡다 **stool** (바 등에 놓는)다리가 긴 의자

· · ·

Rock Bottom Restaurant '아주 저렴한, 소박한 식당' rock bottom은 hit the rock bottom에서 파생된 표현으로 '더 이상 (가격이나 시세 등)내려갈 수 없는 상태'를 의미한다. 때로는 사람의 기분을 표현하기도 한다.

· · ·

Have you been helped?
Not really, may I order now?
주문하셨습니까?
아뇨, 지금 주문해도 될까요?

식당에선 위와 같은 의미로 사용되지만 관공서에서는 '도움을 받으셨나요?'

A Picture of Personal Accountability

It was a beautiful day in downtown Minneapolis when I stopped into a Rock Bottom restaurant for a quick lunch. The place was jammed. I didn't have much time, so I was happy to grab the one stool they had available at the bar. A few minutes after I sat down, a young man carrying a tray full of dirty dishes hurried past on his way to the kitchen, but noticing me out of the corner of his eye, stopped, came back and said, "Sir, have you been helped?"

"No, I haven't," I said, "but all I really want is a salad and a couple of rolls."

"I can get you that, Sir. What would you like to drink?"

"I'll have a Diet Coke, please."

"Oh, I'm sorry, Sir, we sell Pepsi. Would that be all right?"

blur 희미한, 흐릿한 **stir** 휘젓다, 감동시키다 **ounce** 28.35그램 **frosty** 물방울이 맺힌, 서리 내린 **extraordinary** 비상한, 비범한 **wave over** 손을 흔들어 부르다 **be taken aback** 당황하다, 놀라다

• • •

There was a blur of activity off to my left, "wind of enthusiasm" stirred behind me. '내 왼쪽으로 희미한 움직임이 감지되었다. 그것은 내 뒤에서 나를 감동시키는 '열정의 바람'이었다'

over my right shoulder stretched the "long arm of service" '내 오른쪽 어깨 너머로 '긴 서비스의 팔'을 뻗치며'

you guessed it. '네가 생각한(맞춘) 그것' 상대방의 추측을 유도할 때 'you guess(맞혀보세요)'라는 표현을 사용한다.

talk about going extra mile! '더 멀리(깊이) 나아가는 것' 즉 이 사람을 고용하는 것에 그치지 않고 더 심도 있는 부분까지 접근하고 싶다는 의미로 해석할 수 있다.

"Ah, no thanks," I said with a smile, "I'll just have water with lemon, please."

"Great, I'll be back." He disappeared.

Moments later he came back with the salad, the rolls and the water. I thanked him, and he was quickly gone again, leaving me to enjoy my meal, a satisfied customer.

Suddenly, there was a blur of activity off to my left, the "wind of enthusiasm" stirred behind me and then, over my right shoulder stretched the "long arm of service," delivering a twenty-ounce bottle, frosty on the outside, cold on the inside, of—you guessed it—Diet Coke!

"Wow!" I said. "Thank you!"

"You're welcome," he said with a smile, and hurried off again.

My first thought was, "Hire this man!" Talk about going the extra mile! He was clearly not your average employee. But the more I thought about the extraordinary thing he'd just done, the more I wanted to talk to him. So as soon as I could get his attention, I waved him over.

"Excuse me, I thought you didn't sell Coke?" I asked.

"That's right, Sir, we don't."

"Well, where did this come from?"

"The grocery store around the corner, Sir."

I was taken aback.

profound 깊은 **awfully** 대단히, 몹시 **seemingly** 겉으로는 **empowerment** 넘겨진(위임된) 권한, 자격 **but for now** 그러나 일단 지금은

· · ·

Smiling and seemingly growing taller before my eyes. '얼굴에 미소를 머금은 채 뿌듯한 표정으로'
or what? 주로 구두상으로 '그런 것', '뭐 그런 비슷한 것?' 의 의미를 갖는다.
I'll bet 확신을 표현할 때 사용하는 표현이다. 비슷한 표현으로 I'm pretty sure about이 있다.

· · ·

I'm going to ask a doctor to take a look at my shoulder.
Put on your jacket now. I'll give you a ride.
의사한테 내 어깨 좀 봐달라고 해야겠어.
재킷 입어 내가 태워줄게.

take a look at은 look at보다 좀더 정중한 표현이다.

"Who paid for it?" I asked.

"I did, Sir; just a dollar."

By then I was thinking profound and professional thoughts like, "Cool!" But what I said was, "Come on, you've been awfully busy. How did you have time to go get it?" Smiling and seemingly growing taller before my eyes, he said, "I didn't, Sir. I sent my manager!"

I couldn't believe it. Was that empowerment or what? I'll bet we can all think of times we would love to look at our "boss" and say, "Get me a Diet Coke!" What a great image. But beyond that, his actions paint a marvelous picture of personal accountability and The Question Behind the Question. We'll go into the specifics of the QBQ in the chapters to come, but for now let's take a look at my server's thinking and the choices he made.

It was the lunch rush. He was already busy with plenty to do. But he noticed a customer who, though not in his section, looked as though he needed some attention, so he decided to do what he could to help. I don't know what was in his mind at that moment, of course, but faced with a similar situation, many people would have had thoughts like these:

"Why do I have to do everything around here?"

be supposed to ~하기로 되어 있다 short-staffed 직원부족의, 일손이 모자란 lousy 형편없는 refer to ~로 간주하다 implication 함축, 내포 tend to ~하는 경향이 있다 tremendous 거대한, 대단한 contribute 기여하다

"Who's supposed to be covering this area, anyway?"

"When is management going to provide us with more products?"

"Why are we always so short-staffed?"

"When are ustomers going to learn to read the menu?"

It's understandable that someone would feel and think that way, especially when frustrated, but the truth is that these are lousy questions. They're negative and they don't solve any problems. Throughout the rest of the book we'll refer to questions like these as Incorrect Questions, or IQs, since nothing positive or productive comes from asking them. They're also the complete opposite of personal accountability because in each one, the implication is that someone or something else is responsible for the problem or situation.

Unfortunately, though, they're often the first thoughts that come to mind. It's a sad fact that when most of us are faced with a frustration or challenge of some kind, our first reaction tends to be negative and defensive, and the first questions that occur to us are IQs.

The good news is this: That moment of frustration also presents us with a tremendous opportunity to contribute, and the QBQ can help us take advantage of it. The moment

pop into 갑자기 나타나다 **in a nutshell** 요약하면, 간결하게 정리하면 **get caught** ~에 얽매이다, ~에 걸려들다 **downside** 불리한(부정적인) 면

· · ·

he disciplined his thoughts. '그는 자신의 생각들을 바로잡았다'
His choices made the difference. '그의 선택이 차이를 만들었다'
bouncing my quarters across the bar '25센트짜리 동전을 바로 던지면서'
보통 저렴한 식당이나 바에서 '팁을 쿵 하고 내려놓는다'(많이 주었을 때)는 의미의 표현이다.

· · ·

Why only Linda has to deal with the work?
In a nutshell, Linda has to do the work because everyone else is busy.
왜 린다만 그 일을 처리해야 하는 거죠?"
간단히 말해서, 린다는 다른 모든 사람들이 바쁘기 때문에 그 일을 해야 하네.

the IQs pop into our heads, we have a choice. We can either accept them — "Yeah, when are we going to get more help around here?!" — or reject them, choosing instead to ask better, more accountable questions such as, "What can I do to make a difference?" and "How can I support the team?"

This, in a nutshell, is the essence of the QBQ:

Making better choices in the moment by asking better questions.

That's exactly what my server did. He didn't ask IQs and get caught in the downside of the situation. Instead — in the moment — he disciplined his thoughts, made better choices and asked better questions. Whether he used the words or not, his actions clearly indicated accountable thinking such as, "What can I do to help out?" and "How can I provide value to you?" His choices made the difference.

As I left that day, I gave him a good tip, as anyone would have, bouncing my quarters across the bar. (Just kidding. It was the excellent tip he deserved.) And when I returned a couple of months later and asked for "my favorite server, Jacob Miller" — I love his last name — the hostess said, "I'm sorry, Sir, Jacob is no longer ..."

get away 도망가다 **brightly** 밝게, 명랑하게 **toward** ~쪽으로 **management** 회사 임원, 결정권을 갖는 관리자적 지위

• • •

Jacob is no longer··· 보통 직원이 그만두었을 때 'he doesn't work with us any more' 혹은 'he is no longer (work for us) with us' 로 표현한다.
I can't help but think··· '생각할 수 밖에 없다' I can't와 관련된 다음 표현들도 알아두면 좋다. 'I can't help···(어쩔 수 없다)', 'I can't stop···(멈출 수 없다)', 'I can't resist···(~하지 않을 수 없다)'

• • •

How was that movie you told me about?
I couldn't help being bored.
그때 말했던 그 영화는 어땠니?
지루해하지 않을 수 없었어. 그 영화는 세 시간이나 됐거든.

32

My thoughts flew fast, "NO! You lost my own personal server? You lost a guy who looked at me and thought, `What can I do right now to serve you!?'" I just couldn't believe they had let him get away.

But I didn't say any of that to her. I simply interrupted with, "Oh no, you lost him?" to which she brightly responded, "Oh, no Sir, we didn't lose him, he was promoted to management."

My first thought was, "Management, what awaste!" (Go ahead, smile—even if you're a manager.)

The truth is, I wasn't at all surprised that Jacob, with the way he thought, would be so quickly on his way toward his chosen goals. That's the difference personal accountability can make. Everyone wins: customers, coworkers, the organization, everyone. And for Jacob, beyond the tips and the promotion, I can't help but think the greatest win of all is the way he must feel about himself at the end of a day of making better choices, asking better questions and practicing personal accountability.

goat heads '염소머리' 라는 이름을 가진 식물 **wicked little thorns** 작은 가
시가 심하게 많이 나있는(식물) **Upper Midwest combined** 서부 위쪽 주
(states)들 **thick** 두꺼운 **take precautions against** ~을 경계하다, ~에게 미
리 경고하다

· · ·

if one happens to work its way into your shoe. '그 중 하나가 우연히 당신
의 신발 속으로 방향을 잡으면'

· · ·

You have to take precautions when working with chemicals.
Yep. I' ll keep in mind sir.
화학제품을 다룰 때는 조심해야 하네.
네. 명심하겠습니다.

Making Better Choices

Soon after we moved to Denver, we discovered something we'd never seen before: goat heads. Goat heads are wicked little thorns that grow in this part of the country and have what look like the ears, horns and nose of a goat. They fall to the ground with their horns pointing in the air, and if one happens to work its way into your shoe—or your bike tire—it can really ruin your day.

In fact, if you live in the West, it will come as no surprise to you that we've changed more bicycle tires since moving here than during all the years combined that we lived in the Upper Midwest combined. Serious bikers take multiple precautions against goat heads for even the thickest mountain—bike tires.

Each day, as we journey into the unexplored wilds of our

countless 셀 수 없는 **procrastination** 미루는 버릇, 지연 **fundamental** 기
본적인, 기초의

• • •

a big step toward making great things happen in our lives. '우리 삶에
좋은 일이 생기게 만들어준 큰 진보'

personal and professional lives, we have countless choices to make. And what are we choosing? Not our next action, but our next thought. Choose the wrong thought and we're off into the emotional goat heads of blame, complaining and procrastination. But the right thoughts lead us to a richer, more fulfilling life and the feelings of pride and accomplishment that come from making productive decisions.

The idea that we are accountable for our own choices and are free to make better ones is fundamental to the QBQ. Sometimes people think they have no choice.

They'll say things like, "I have to" or "I can't." But we always have a choice. Always. Even deciding not to choose is making a choice. Realizing this and taking responsibility for our choices is a big step toward making great things happen in our lives.

Want to avoid the goat heads and make great things happen?

Make better choices.

built on ~을 기반으로 세워지다 **observation** 관찰 **initial** 처음의 **guiding principle** 기본 원칙, 원리

· · ·

But how can we tell a good question from a bad one? '하지만 우리가 어떻게 나쁜 질문과 좋은 질문을 구분할 수 있을까?' 여기서 tell은 '분간하다', '구분하다' 의 뜻으로 쓰인다.

QBQ! The Question Behind the Question

Now let's talk about the tool that brings personal accountability to life: the QBQ.

The Question Behind the Question is built on the observation that our first reactions are often negative, bringing to mind Incorrect Questions (IQs). But if in each moment of decision we can instead discipline our thoughts to look behind those initial questions and ask better ones (QBQs), the questions themselves will lead us to better results.

One of the guiding principles of the QBQ is, "The answers are in the questions," which speaks to the same truth: If we ask a better question, we get a better answer. So the QBQ is about asking better questions. But how can we tell a good question from a bad one? What does a "better"

facet (다면체, 특히 보석의) 한 면

. . .

But don't let its simplicity fool you. '하지만 그 단순함에 속지 않도록 하게'

. . .

Don't let its simplicity fool you.
I see what you're getting at. But it's not going to be happen.
그 단순함에 속지 않도록 하게.
무슨 말씀을 하시는지 알겠습니다. 하지만 그런 일은 없을 겁니다.

question look like?

This book will help each of us learn to recognize and ask better questions. For starters, here are the three simple guidelines for creating a QBQ.

1. Begin with "What" or "How" (**not** "Why," "When" or "Who")
2. Contain an "I" (**not** "they," "them," "we" or "you")
3. Focus on action.

"What can I do?" for example, follows the guidelines perfectly. It begins with "What," contains an "I" and focuses on action: "What can I do?" Simple, as I said. But don't let its simplicity fool you. Like a jewel, the QBQ is made up of many facets. In the following chapters, we'll explore these facets and see the powerful effect asking QBQs can have on our lives.

aloud 소리 내어 **powerless** 무기력함   **tone** 말투, 어조   **victim** 희생자
quick point 여기서 잠깐

Chapter Four

Don't Ask "Why?"

Ever heard these questions:

"Why don't others work harder?"

"Why is this happening to me?"

"Why do they make it so difficult for me to do my job?"

Say them aloud. How do they make you feel? When I say them, I feel powerless, like a victim. Questions with a "Why me?" tone to them say, "I'm a victim of the environment and the people around me." Not a very productive thought, is it? But we ask them all the time.

(Quick point: If you've been trained on the "Five Whys" of problem solving or selling, that's not what we're talking about here. Those are useful and appropriate. What we're referring to

classic pity party 뻔한 동정파티(위로하는 자리나 모임) **undoubtedly** 의심할 여지없이, 확실히 **victim thinking** 피해의식 **second home** (주말, 휴가용의) 별장 **Aspen** 스위스의 지역 이름 **discretionary income** 재량소득(매우 많은 수입을 의미) **broker** 부동산, 보험 등의 중계자 **personal injury attorney** 개인 상해, 손해 변호사 **opt** 고르다

• • •

Poor me. '동정을 바라거나 자신이 불쌍하다(혹은 한심하다)' 라는 의미로 해석할 수 있다.

It's a funny line··· 여기서 line은 '대사' 나 '말(言)' 등을 의미한다.

conversation along the lines of '다음의 말이 포함된 대화'

Guess what he does '그 사람이 뭐 하는지 맞춰봐' 구어체 상에서 guess와 의문사(what, when, where, how, who, why···etc)가 쓰이면 '추측해보라, 맞추어 보라' 는 의미가 된다.

are questions that begin with "Why" and have the "poor me" tone that leads straight to the classic pity party.)

Anyone can fall into the "Why" trap. I asked a department manager once how many people worked for him, and he said, "About half!" It's a funny line, but he was undoubtedly the kind of manager who would also ask the IQs, "Why can't I find good people?" "Why doesn't the younger generation really want to work?" "Why don't I get more direction from upper management?"

That's all victim thinking, and there's too much of it in the world already.

I was on a long flight, sitting next to a man in his mid-fifties. We introduced ourselves, and started a friendly conversation along the lines of, "Where are you heading?" and "What do you do?" It turns out he owns a second home near Aspen and was just returning from a twenty-one–day ski vacation. "Wow!" I thought. "Twenty-one days in Aspen. This man has some discretionary income!" He went on to say he lives in New York City and works on Wall Street. Guess what he does. He's not a broker. He's a personal injury attorney.

When he asked me what I do, I opted for the quick, easy answer, "Author, speaker." "Oh really?" he said. "What do you speak about?" I considered this for a moment and

fidget 안절부절 못하다 **be made up of** ~로 구성되어 있다 **get rid of** 제거
하다

· · ·

wondering if he'd see the irony and humor. '그 사람이 그 아이러니와 유
머를 알게 될지 궁금해' 개인 상해관련 변호사는 상대방에게 때로는 부당한 청
구를 하기 때문에 저자의 직업과 상충되는 면이 있을 수 있다. 그 점이 우습고
아이러니 하다는 것이다.
I have nothing against him. '나는 그에 대한 악감정은 없다'
But even as we shake our heads about the ills of society. '하지만 우리가
사회의 병폐에 대해 고개를 내저을지라도' shake one's head는 '(실망, 불응 등
의 몸짓으로)고개를 젓다' 라는 뜻이다.

· · ·

I was wondering if I could use your phone.
Absolutely. Here it is.
전화 좀 사용해도 될지 모르겠네요.
당연하죠. 여기 있어요.

thought, "Why not?" So I said what I always say, "Personal accountability," wondering if he'd see the irony and the humor. It took a couple of moments. We stared at each other. He fidgeted a bit. Finally, just to be clear, I added, "What I really do is help people—including myself—eliminate victim thinking from their lives." He must have understood me then because he got up and moved and we never spoke again!

I have nothing against him or his profession. He's simply providing what's demanded by a culture that continually asks, "Why is this happening to me?" But even as we shake our heads about the ills of society, let's not forget that society is made up of individuals. You and me. The best thing we can do to get rid of victim thinking in our world is to get rid of it in ourselves.

The first QBQ guideline says, all QBQs begin with "What" or "How," not "Why," "When" or "Who." Take another look at the "Why" questions at the beginning of the chapter and consider what would happen if we asked these instead:

"How can I do my job better today?"
"What can I do to improve the situation?"
"How can I support others?"

something go wrong 무언가가 잘못되다 **civilian life** (군 생활과 반대로)민간
생활 **territory** 영업상의 구역 **go through** ~을 통과하다, ~에 참가하다
in- house 사내(조직)에서의

Chapter Five

The Victim

I received an e-mail from a gentleman who wrote that during his 10 years in the military, whenever something went wrong, the only acceptable response was, "No excuses, Sir!" He accepted it, he believed it and he lived it.

When he returned to civilian life, he started working as a territory manager for a large firm in the food industry. He wasn't doing as well as his company expected, and he wasn't pleased with his own performance, either. The day before he went through an in-house training program on personal accountability and the QBQ, he had gone to his manager and asked questions like these:

"Why don't you give me more of your time?"
"Why don't you coach me more?"

slip into ~로 빠지다, 미끄러져 들어가다 **no wonder** ~하는 것은 당연하다
lookout 경계, 조심

• • •

I'm frustrated with the whole process.
No excuse!
모든 과정이 실망스럽네요.
변명의 여지가 없습니다!

no excuse는 보통 자기 잘못을 직접적으로 시인하거나 인정할 때 자주 표현된다.

"Why aren't we more competitive?"

"Why don't we get some new products?"

"Why doesn't marketing support us more?"

He closed his e-mail saying, "I realized when I learned the QBQ that from military to business, in just a few short years, I had become what I hated the most: the victim." If this man, after 10 years of living and breathing "No excuses!" can slip into victim thinking, it's no wonder the rest of us have to be on the lookout for it in our own lives.

stress out 스트레스 받다　**struggle** 분투하다　**tumble** 넘어지다, 폭락하다
follow through (업무, 계획 등) 완수하다

• • •

The economy sours… '경제는 불황이고' sour는 '맛이 시다' 의 의미와 더불어 '좋지 않다' 라는 의미도 있다.
trigger event '결정적, 중요한 사건' trigger는 '방아쇠' 또는 '중요한 문제를 야기하는 것' 의 의미로 사용된다.

• • •

Do you buy that?
That's out of the question.
그것을 인정하십니까?
그건 말도 안 됩니다.

buy는 보통 '사다, 구매하다' 의 의미이지만 '～을 믿다, 받아들이다' 의 의미도 있다.

52

"Why is this happening to me?"

Stress is a choice. Do you buy that? Some people have a hard time with the idea. They think it's the people and events in our lives that stress us out—management, colleagues, customers, the boss, traffic, weather, market conditions—but it isn't true.

Yes, bad things happen: The economy sours, our business struggles, the stock market tumbles, jobs are lost, people around us don't follow through, deadlines are missed, projects fail, good people leave. Life is full of these. But still, stress is a choice because whatever the "trigger event," we always choose our own response. We choose to react angrily. We choose to stuff our emotions and keep quiet. We choose to worry. (One client had a sign on his desk that said, "I've had many problems, some of which

the result of ~의 결과 **have no control** (통제력)자제력이 없는 **mindset** (고정된)사고방식, 태도

. . .

They have no control over their son.
I see. That's why their son is so spoiled.
그들은 자기 아들에 대한 통제력이 전혀 없어.
아, 알겠어요. 그래서 그 애가 그렇게 버릇이 없는 거군요.

came true!") Different people have different reactions to the same situation. Stress is a choice.

Stress is also the result of our choices. When we choose to ask a question like, "Why is this happening to me?" we feel as if we have no control. This leads us to a victim mindset, which is extremely stressful. Even in cases where we actually are victims and our feelings seem justified, "Why me?" thinking only adds to our stress.

take off 이륙하다 **joy-ride** 재미로 하는 비행 **Cessna** 미국의 세스나 항공기 회사가 생산하는 경비행기 **abrupt halt** 갑작스런 멈춤 **reassuring tone** 조용하고 안심시키는 어조로 **repertoire** 레퍼토리, 목록

• • •

Not long into the flight ‘비행을 시작한지 오래 지나지 않아’
What works one day in a given situation does not necessarily work the next. ‘어떤 상황에서 잠시 효과가 있더라도 다음에도 반드시 효과가 있는 것은 아니다’ one day는 ‘잠시 또는 잠깐’의 의미이다.

Chapter Seven

"Why do we have to go through all this change?"

When Stacey was 12 years old, she and her father, a pilot, took off on a Sunday afternoon joy-ride in their single-engine Cessna. Not long into the flight, and about a mile up over Lake Michigan, the joy of their father-daughter adventure came to an abrupt halt. The engine quit.

Stacey's father turned to her and in a calm, reassuring tone said, "Honey, the engine has quit. I'm going to need to fly the plane differently." Interesting phrase: "Fly the plane differently."

Her father understood that new challenges and changing conditions often require different strategies. Conditions change, markets change, people change. What works one day in a given situation does not necessarily work the next. We need to develop a repertoire of responses so we're

cockpit 조정석 **sensing the gravity** 중력(여기서는 위험상황)을 느끼며 **go off** 벗어나다, 떠나다 **oxymoron** 모순적인 말을 구사하는 것 **dive** (비행기, 새 등이)급강하하다 **fiddle with** 계속 손으로 다루다(조작하다) **level off** (순항고도에 이르러)수평 비행으로 옮기는 조작을 하다 **sputters** 탁탁 소리(기계음)를 내다 **hum** (기계 등이) 윙윙거리다 **pat** 토닥거리다

· · ·

This did not go off to the headquarters for a committee decision—a term that always strikes me as an oxymoron. 직역하면 '이는 위원회의 결정에 대한 본사의 방침에서 벗어나지 않는다—나를 모순적인 것으로 공격했던 그 기간 중' 이 된다. 즉, 그러한 예(this)는 저자의 회사 본사에서도 있었는데 저자가 위원회의 결정을 따르지 않았기 때문에 말도 안 되는 일로 공격당했다는 뜻이다.

Hang on! '꽉 잡아!' 보통 자동차나 비행기 등의 속도를 낼 때 자주 들을 수 있는 말이다. 전화상에서는 '기다리세요' 라는 의미도 있다.

Rock of Gibraltar '지르롤터의 바위' 에스파냐와 안달루시아 지방에 이어져 있는 바위로 2차 세계대전 때 철통의 요새로 알려졌다.

first with just a few hopeful sputters, but finally with a secure, familiar hum. '처음에는 맥없이 탁탁 거리는 소리뿐이었지만 마침내 안정된 기계소리가 났다'

prepared when our engine unexpectedly quits.

In order to restart the engine, they needed more air speed. Stacey's father told her he would be hitting switches in the cockpit while he steered the plane downward. ("Toward the deep, cold waters of Lake Michigan!" I thought as she told me the story.) Stacey understood, and, sensing the gravity of the situation, quickly nodded her approval of Dad's plan. (This did not go off to the headquarters for a committee decision—a term that always strikes me as an oxymoron.)

Her father put the plane into a dive and fiddled with the switches, but nothing happened. He leveled off closer to the water. "Stacey, we're going to try that again," he said. "Hang on!" They dove a second time. He hit the switches again as the plane gained speed and this time the engine fired, first with just a few hopeful sputters, but finally with a secure, familiar hum.

About 20 minutes later, they landed safely. At that point, this Rock of Gibraltar kind of guy, this Fearless Father, this Man of Courage turned to his twelve-year-old daughter, lovingly patted her shoulder and said, "Now honey, whatever you do, don't tell Mom!"

I love this story. Not just for the drama and the humor, but for what it says about handling change. When faced

resist 저항하다, 거부하다 **whining** 징징거리다 **adapt** 적응시키다

· · ·

Here's one that really works. '여기 정말로 효과 있는 질문이 있다'

with a new situation, Stacey's dad took action and solved the problem. But if he had resisted the change and instead spent his time whining and complaining, having thoughts like, "Well, I've never done it that way before!" or asking IQs such as, "Why do we have to go through all this change?" things might have turned out much differently.

Are you facing change? Any engines quit in your life lately? If so, ask a better question. Here's one that really works: "How can I adapt to the changing world?"

facilitate (일을)순조롭게 진행하다 **over and over again** 끊임없이, 계속

· · ·

What's the critical issue facing your organization today? '현재 당신 조직이 직면하고 있는 가장 큰 문제는 무엇입니까?'
It's framed like this. '그것은 이와 같은 형태이다'

Chapter Eight

"Why don't they communicate better?"

In the many workshops I've facilitated over the years, this scene has played out over and over again: I'll ask, "What's the critical issue facing your or ganization today?" Generally, the answer is not change or competition, but communication. Then it's framed like this: "Why don't they communicate better?"

Actually, communication does not only mean being understood, but also understanding the other person. The QBQ is, "How can I better understand you?"

Understand?

put off 미루다 **procrastination** 태만, 연기 **hard-core** 변하지 않는, 강경파
sneaky 몰래 하는, 비열한

• • •

Sorry, but would you call me back one hour later?
Sure, then I'll call you back at 11:00.
죄송하지만 1시간 뒤에 다시 전화 주시겠습니까?
물론이죠, 그럼 11시에 다시 전화 드리겠습니다.

Chapter Nine

Don't Ask "When?"

"When will they take care of the problem?"

"When will the customer call me back?"

"When will we get the information we need to make a decision?"

When we ask "When?" we're really saying we have no choice but to wait and put off action until another time. Questions that begin with "When" lead to procrastination.

I don't believe most people intend to procrastinate. Certainly no one ever gets out of bed and says, "Today, I'm going to procrastinate!" (Even a hard-core procrastinator who might want to say all that, would put it off until tomorrow.) But procrastination is a sneaky problem. We put something off until a little later, and then a little later, and a little later

postpone 강조하다, 뒤로 미루다 **hesitate** 주저하다 **consequence** 결과, 결
말 **long range vision** 장기적인 안목 **get something done** ~을 마치다, 끝
내다 **feel overwhelmed** 압도되는 느낌을 받다, 부담감을 느끼다 **bottom
line** 결론 **externally** 외부(외면)적인

• • •

Procrastination is costly to all involved. '미루기는 모든 면에 영향을 미
친다'

again until, before we know it, the action has been postponed so long that it has become a serious problem.

Is any procrastination going on in your life? Most people don't hesitate to admit that procrastination is a problem for them. And if it's a problem for most people, it's also a problem for most organizations. What are the consequences? Putting things off means precious time is lost. Productivity suffers. The team may not progress toward its goal. Deadlines are missed.

As a client once said, "Long-range vision and strategic planning are great tools, but we need to get somethings done before lunch!"

Procrastination also increases stress. As things pile up, we begin to feel overwhelmed, which takes the joy out of our work. Bottom line: Procrastination is costly to all involved.

Why do we do it? I'm sure there are reasons we could explore, but frankly, I'd prefer to talk about solutions. And one solution is to stop asking externally focused questions that begin with "When?" Instead, we need to ask QBQs such as:

"What solution can I provide?"
"How can I more creatively reach the customer?"

Remember : The answers are in the questions. '기억하라 : 해답은 항상
그 문제 안에 있다'

"What can I do to find the info to make a decision?"

Remember: The answers are in the questions.

give away 무료로 주다 **toped with** ~이 위에 놓인 **quarter** 4분의 1 **feet** 길이의 단위(약 30.48센티미터) **lean against** ~에 기대다 **hoop pole** 쇠기둥 **at the edge of** ~의 가장자리에 **yell** 소리치다, 고함치다 **glance at** 흘끔 보다 **trimming bushes** 나무 가지를 깎아 다듬기 **garage** 차고 **blow over** 바람에 (넘어가다)쓰러지다

· · ·

three feet by five feet '가로 3피트, 세로 5피트의 크기'

Chapter Ten

Procrastination:
The Friend of Failure

I decided to give away a very large, old wooden desk, topped with a piece of quarter-inch-thick clear glass, about three feet by five feet. The new owner didn't want the glass. When we loaded the desk into his truck early one Saturday morning, we left the sheet of glass leaning against the basketball hoop pole at the edge of our driveway.

As my friend drove away with the desk, he said, "You'd better put that glass in a safe place." I yelled back, "I will!" But I didn't. I glanced at it and told myself I'd do it later. Then I got busy trimming bushes and cleaning the garage. Every time I walked by that sheet of glass, I told myself that I should move it before it blew over. I'll do it later, I kept thinking.

at dusk 해질 무렵에 **spot** 발견하다 **grass clipper** 잔디 깎기 **curb** 인도의 모서리 **street light** 가로등 **shatter** 산산조각 나다 **dash out** 급히 가다, 튀어 나가다 **atop** ~의 꼭대기에 **shards of glass** 유리 파편들 **porch** 현관 **pavement** 포장도로

• • •

The day wore on ‘날이 지나고’ wear on은 ‘(시간이)지나가다, 경과하다’ 라는 뜻을 갖는다.
Off he went as I headed into the house. go off는 ‘출발, 착수’를 의미하는 구어적 표현으로 전치사 off가 문장 앞으로 도치되었다. 해석하면 ‘내가 집 쪽으로 향하자 그도 일(잔디 깎기를 치우는)을 시작했다’

• • •

I think it became hotter as the day wore on.
Yea, summer's coming now.
날이 지날수록 더 더워지는 것 같아.
네, 여름이 오고 있는 거죠.

The day wore on and we decided to go out to dinner as a family. As we backed out of the driveway, my wife, Karen, said, "Shouldn't we put that glass someplace safe?" You know what I told her.

A couple of hours later we arrived home at dusk, and were all heading into the house when I spotted a small pair of grass clippers sitting near the curb under a street light. I said to our son, Michael, who was nine, "Mike, would you go over there and grab those clippers and put them in the garage for me, please?" Off he went as I headed into the house.

It was a quiet Saturday evening in our pleasant neighborhood, until the silence was broken by the most terrifying sound I have ever heard: the shattering of a large piece of plate glass.

I realized instantly what had happened. I also knew why. I dashed out of the garage and around our car to find Michael lying in the driveway on his stomach atop hundreds of deadly shards of glass, some more than a foot long. He was crying as I ran, carrying him, to the front porch. I held him under the light to check his injuries, expecting the worst, and I couldn't believe what I saw: not a scratch! He had run right into the glass and fallen on top of it as it hit the pavement, but there wasn't a mark on him.

understatement 말로 표현하지 못할 정도로   **explode into** 확 ~하다   **ca-tastrophe** 큰 재앙(참사)

• • •

Let's take care of the little things while they're still little. '사소한 일은 그 일이 아직 사소할 때 처리하자'

To say we felt incredibly thankful would be an under-statement.

Why did this incident happen? Procrastination, the Friend of Failure. I knew the glass needed to be put away, and doing so would have taken no more than a few minutes. But I put it off and put it off until finally it exploded into what could have been a catastrophe.

Let's take care of the little things while they're still little.

imperfect 완벽하지 않은, 불완전한 **finite** 한정된, 유한의

• • •

Hitting target. '목표를 달성하는 것'
Creativity is thinking outside the box. '창의성은 자신의 틀을 벗어난 사고이다' 많은 격언에는 box란 단어가 등장한다. 여기서 box란 '현실' 혹은 '자기만의 세계', '틀' 과 같은 추상적인 의미로 사용된다.

Chapter Eleven

"When will we get more tools and better systems?"

Most of us have heard the saying, "Creativity is thinking outside the box." There's a lot of truth in that, but to me true creativity is this:

Succeeding with in the box.

Hitting targets, reaching goals, doing the job well and making a difference with what we already have is the QBQ way. Every organization has imperfect systems and finite resources. We may wish we had newer tools, better systems, more people and bigger budgets. But thinking too much about what we'd like to have is another cause of procrastination. Managers for example, won't take their group through team-building until "all the right people are

State Farm Insurance 미국의 주택, 자동차 전문 보험사

• • •

We sow, then we reap. '씨를 뿌린 만큼 거둔다'

in place." Individuals won't make a decision until they have all the information, or take action until all the questions are answered.

Ironically, succeeding with what we have makes us more likely to get the things we wanted in the first place. Listen to the wisdom of Deb Weber from State Farm Insurance: "I find that every time I do the job with the tools I have, I tend to receive more tools." It's a truth: We sow, then we reap.

Focusing on what we don't have is a waste of time and energy. To really make a difference, let's instead focus our energy on succeeding within the box. Let's ask the QBQ, "How can I achieve with the resources I already have?"

profession 전문직 **complicate** 복잡한 **fundamental** 기본, 기초 **prospective clients** 유망 고객들 **following up** 계속 상황을 지켜보는 것
shortage 부족

Chapter Twelve

"When are we going to hear something new?"

Sales can be a difficult profession, but it is not complicated. If salespeople consistently practice the fundamentals—getting up early, contacting prospective clients, sharing their belief in the value of their products and services, following up—they'll be successful.

But I can't tell you how many times sales people have come up and asked something like, "John, I've taken Selling Skills 101. What's next?" My answer? "NOTHING!" The problem is not a shortage of new ideas, but a lack of understanding that the "old" ideas still work.

This may not be true with technology, which changes every five minutes, but when it comes to the principles on which we can base our organizations and lives, the old stuff is the good stuff.

day in and day out 날마다, 평소에

. . .

How often in our organization have we brought in the 'blue' program, the 'red' program, and the 'green' program — all inside of ninety days — only to have them make little difference anyway. '우리는 얼마나 자주 조직에 여러 가지 프로그램(이 모든 것을 3개월 안에)을 도입하는가, 그 프로그램들 간에 별 차이도 없는데도 불구하고 말이다' blue, red, green이라는 색을 사용해 프로그램을 구분한 것은 다양하기만 할 뿐 차이는 없는 프로그램을 빗대기 위함이다.

. . .

My dog wakes me up at 5AM day in and day out.
Really? I wish I could have a dog just like yours.
매일 아침 5시가 되면 나의 개가 나를 깨우지.
정말? 나도 그런 개를 가질 수 있었으면 좋겠어.

How often in our organizations have we brought in the "blue" program, the "red" program and the "green" program—all inside of 90 days—only to have them make little difference anyway because there are no quick fixes for long—term problems? We don't need the "new" thing or the "hot" topic. What we need to do is practice the fundamentals—like personal accountability—day in and day out.

"When are we going to hear something new?" is the wrong question. The right one is, "How can I apply what I'm hearing?"—even if I've heard it before.

scapegoat 희생양 **pervasive** 그르치는, 악용하는   **counterproductive** 비생산적인 **so far** 지금까지 **flip toward** 책장을 넘기다 **internal identity** 조직의 정체성

· · ·

Company Coat of Arms '기업의 문장(紋章)' coat of arms란 옛날 기사들이 갑옷 위에 입은 문장을 의미한다.

· · ·

He's been made a scapegoat for their lack of success.
Well, I wouldn't do that if I were him.
그는 그들의 실패에 대한 희생양을 만들고 말았지.
글쎄. 나라면 그처럼 하진 않았을 꺼야.

Chapter Thirteen

Don't Ask "Who?"

"Who made the mistake?"

"Who missed the deadline?"

"Who dropped the ball?"

When we ask "Who" questions like these, what we're really doing is looking for scapegoats, someone else to blame. And blame may well be the most pervasive and counterproductive of all the ideas we've talked about so far. Flip forward to the image on page 86: arms crossed, fingers pointed at everyone else. I call this the "Company Coat of Arms." If organizations had separate logos to represent their internal identities, too often this would be it.

While riding in a van from Snowbird Ski Resort in Utah

strike up a conversation 대화를 시작하다 **receptionist** 접수원 **dis-patcher** 운항관리원 **lowest rung on the ladder** 사다리의 가장 아랫단 **epidemic** 유행(전염)성의 **immune** 면역의 **on and on** 계속해서, 쉬지 않고 **circle of blame** 비난의 악순환

· · ·

I have a hard time striking up a conversation with a stranger.
But you are the first secretary, you have to get used to it.
나는 낯선 사람들과 대화하는 게 힘들어.
하지만 넌 수석 비서잖아. 익숙해져야 해.

to the Salt Lake City airport, I struck up a conversation with the driver. Turned out he doubled as the sales manager for th transportation firm. As we talked about the subject of blame, he said, "Oh, we've got lots of blame going on in our company!"

"Really?" I said, hoping he'd go on.

"Yeah," he continued. "The receptionist blames the dispatchers, who blame the drivers, who blame the sales people, who blame me..."

I stopped him. "How many people are in your firm?"

"Twelve," he said. Twelve people! I guess you don't have to be big to play the blame game.

From the smallest group to the largest corporation, from the lowest rung on the ladder to the highest office in the land, there's an epidemic of blame going on and no one seems immune. The CEO blames the vice president, who blames the manager, who blames the employee, who blames the customer, who blames the government, who blames the people, who blame the politicians, who blame the schools, who blame the parents, who blame the teen, who blames the dad, who blames the mom, who blames her manager, who blames the vice president, who blames the CEO, and on and on it goes. This is the "Circle of Blame," and it would be kind of funny if it weren't so true.

potential 가능한, 잠재하는

· · ·

whodunit '추리극(소설)' 여기서는 비난의 대상이 '누구' 인지 모르는 상황을 빗대어 한 말이다.

blamestorm '끊임없이 비난하다' brainstorming을 빗대어 만든 말이다.

What action can I take to 'own' the situation? 직역하면 '상황을 소유하기 위해 어떤 행동을 취해야 할까?' 즉, 상황을 소유한다는 것은 상황을 통제한다는 것의 비유적 표현이다.

Blame and "whodunit" questions solve nothing. They create fear, destroy creativity and build walls. Instead of brainstorming and working together to get things done, we blamestorm and accomplish nothing. There's not a chance we'll reach our full potential until we stop blaming each other and start practicing personal accountability.

"What can I do today to solve the problem?"
"How can I help move the project forward?"
"What action can I take to 'own' the situation?"

Try these questions instead of the "Who?" questions at the beginning of this chapter, and see how fast you can break the Circle of Blame in your organization.

Let's have some fun and carry this idea further. '재미 삼아 이 아이디어를 좀더 진척시켜보자'

Whom do accountable people blame? '책임감 있는 사람들이 비난하는 사람은 누구인가?'

Chapter Fourteen

A Poor Sailor Blames the Wind

Have you ever heard the saying, "A poor sailor blames the wind?" How about, "A poor worker blames the tool," or "A poor coach blames the players?" Let's have some fun and carry this idea further:

A poor teacher blames the _______________.

A poor salesperson blames the _______________.

A poor parent blames the _______________.

A poor manager blames the _______________.

A poor employee blames the _______________.

A poor coach blames the _______________.

A poor teenager blames the—world!

Whom do accountable people blame? No one. Not even themselves.

we/they syndrome 우리/그들(우리가 아닌 사람들)로 양분하는 행동양식
cross functional friction 서로 다른 업무분야 간의 알력, 충돌 **versus** 대(對)
mentality 지력, 지성 **smirk** 능글맞은 웃음 **imply** 포함하다, 내포하다 **executive** 보통 회사의 결정권이 있는 관리직, ex)C.E.O(Chief Executive Officer)

· · ·

field-versus-corporate mentality '현장과 본사의 생각 차이' 여기서 field는
현장직을 의미한다.

Chapter Fifteen

Silos

"You're kidding!" I said. "You don't have a 'we/they' syndrome here?" Kevin, a vice president of operations sat smiling and shaking his head as I continued. "No cross-functional friction? No field-versus-corporate mentality? No management-versus-employees attitude? No 'we/they' ?!" I couldn't believe it. If it were true, his would be the first organization I'd ever seen that didn't have this problem.

"Nope," he said and added with a smirk, "There's no 'we/they' here. But it is 'us against them!' "

Kevin was having a little fun. "Of course," his joke implied, "of course we have a 'we/they' syndrome. Who doesn't?"

I met another executive who had a more direct way of

sum up 요약, 적요 **in some way** 어떻게 해서든 **overdue** 기한이 지난 **cross purposes** 교차된 목표들, 즉 '같은 목표' **so-called** 소위 **bicker** 말다 툼하다 **compartmentalization** 구획화, 구별화 **infighting** 내분 **drain** 고갈 시키다, 소모시키다 **tandem bike** 2인용 자전거 **exertion** 노력, 분발

• • •

silos and buttcovering silo는 곡식 등을 쌓아두는 건물이나 지하 격납고 등 뜻하지만 여기에서는 조직 속 각각의 배타적 집단을 의미한다. 또한 buttco-vering은 '엉덩이를 가린다' 즉, 자기 앞가림에만 급급한 행태를 의미한다.

I know of one company whose field sales organization actually refers to its own headquarters as the 'Sales Prevention Club'! '내가 아는 어느 기업의 지역 영업소에서는 본사를 '영업 방해 단체' 라고 여길 정도였다'

This kind of compartmentalization and infighting drains the life right out of an organization. '이러한 구획화와 내부 갈등이 조직의 생명을 고갈시 킨다'

94

putting it: "John, I can sum up all our problems in a few words: 'silos and buttcovering.' "

Do you have silos in your organization, called accounting, sales, manufacturing, marketing, R&D, operations, administration, the home office or the field? Can people be heard claiming in some way, "That's not my job," while the walls grow taller, stronger and more difficult to overcome? I know of one company whose field sales organization actually refers to its own headquarters as the "Sales Prevention Club!" Then there was the customer service person at a specialty catalog house (I'd called in to check on an overdue order) who told me, "Yeah, the shipping department is doing it to us again!" Us? Whose team does she think she's on?

For all the time and resources our organizations spend on team-building, we still seem to forget one simple truth: We're all on the same team. Every day, we see groups, departments, regions and individuals work at cross purposes. Our so-called teams bicker and complain about the "others" who don't "do their jobs right." This kind of compartmentalization and infighting drains the life right out of an organization. It's like having a tandem bike with the riders facing in opposite directions: lots of activity, lots of exertion, but no forward movement.

afford to ~할 수 있을 만큼 **climb out of** ~에서 기어 나오다

• • •

It's a long story, but to sum it up, we're going to have to move our office to a new town next year.
That's a good idea! We can have more business possibility there.
긴 얘기지만 요약하면 내년에 새 도시로 우리 사무실을 이전해야 한다는 거야.
좋은 생각이군, 거기서 사업성을 좀더 넓힐 수 있을 거야.

With competitors working to beat us every day, can we really afford to be working against each other, too? Let's climb out of our silos, forget the "we/they", and remember: We're all on the same team.

mat (레슬링)매트   **opponent** 적수, 상대   **referee** 심판원(줄여서 Ref.)
overtime 연장전   **questionable calls** 문제가 될 만한(미심 쩍은)판정
conclude 결론짓다

· · ·

It doesn't matter how close the match is. '점수차가 얼마나 적은지는 문제
가 되지 않는다'
man in black and white 검은색과 흰색 유니폼 입은 심판을 표현한 말이기
도 하나 판정을 흑백으로 내린다는 의미. 하지만 일반적으론 '문서에 기록한'
의 의미로 사용된다.
If you want to win, you must be good enough to beat the ref! '네가 이기
길 원한다면 심판을 이길 수 있을 정도로 잘해야 한다'

· · ·

**It says right here in black and white that your company has to pay the
insurance. Do you still think I'm lying?**
I guess you're right.
보험료는 당신 회사에서 부담한다고 바로 여기에 적혀 있습니다. 아직도 제가
거짓말한다고 생각하십니까?
당신이 맞는 것 같네요.

Chapter Sixteen

Beat the Ref

My father, Jimmy Miller, was head wrestling coach at Cornell University in Ithaca, N.Y., for more than 25 years. When he sent me out to the mat, he'd always remind me I had three people to beat that day: my opponent, myself and the referee.

That I had to beat my opponent was obvious. By "myself" he meant I had to overcome the fears any athlete naturally has. About beating the ref, he'd say, "It doesn't matter how close the match is, John. Even if you lose in overtime by one point, even if he makes a couple of questionable calls, you cannot blame the man in black and white." He'd conclude by saying, "If you want to win, you must be good enough to beat the ref!"

Good enough to beat the ref. That means being a sales-

maturity 성숙함, 원숙 **pull one's weight** 제 몫을 하다, 역할(임무)을 다하다
beyond control 통제하에 있지 않은 **supervisor** 일반적으로 직장의 상사
inefficient 효과적이지 못한 **sap** 수액을 짜내다, ~의 활력을 잃게 하다
overcome 극복하다 **barrier** 장애, 장벽

· · ·

I was outsold. '나는 남들보다 많이 팔았다' 즉 한계에 다다를 정도로 최선
을 다했다.
Why don't others pull their own weight? '왜 다른 사람들은 자신의 역할
을 다하지 못할까?' pull one's weight는 '제 역할을 다하다' 라는 뜻이다.

· · ·

**We're planning a surprise party for boss, so no mater what, don't let
him know!**
Yep. I'll go along with you.
우린 지금 사장님을 위한 깜짝 파티를 준비중이야. 어떠한 일이 있어도 알려지
면 안돼!
네. 저도 그렇게 할게요.

person who has the maturity to say, "I was outsold," instead of complaining about product, price and the lack of advertising. It means serving as a team member who never says, "Why don't others pull their own weight?" It means being a manager who doesn't complain, "Why aren't my people motivated?" It means being people who don't complain about management saying, "Why don't they tell us what's going on?"

Who is the "ref" in your life? What person or situation beyond your control is standing between you and success? Could it be a supervisor who over-manages, making it difficult for you to do your job, or inefficient systems built into your organization that waste a lot of your time? Or maybe it's a personal situation that

saps your energy.

No matter what we're trying to accomplish, there's always a barrier of some kind to overcome, and it's often something over which we have no control. Instead of focusing on the barriers, let's work to become so good that we'll succeed no matter how many bad calls the ref may throw at us.

If you want to win, don't complain about things beyond your control. Just be good enough to beat the ref.

humid 습한 **steamy** 후끈한 **cabin** (비행기의)객실 **overbooked** 초과 예약
된 **carry-on luggage** (객실에 들고 탈수 있는)여행가방 **mercifully**(문장 전체를
수식할 경우)다행히도

• • •

Tension in the cabin was high. '객실에는 높은 긴장감이 감돌았다'
We taxied to the runway. '우리는 활주로로 실려갔다' taxi가 동사로 표현
될 때에는 '비행기가 이동하다', '택시로 나르다' 라는 의미를 갖는다. 여기서
는 승객들이 짐짝 취급받는 모습을 묘사했다.

Chapter Seventeen

"Who dropped the ball?"

It was a humid day in Houston. As I boarded the plane, I could feel the heat in the steamy, crowded cabin. The flight was obviously overbooked, and every passenger seemed to have three pieces of large carry-on luggage. On top of that, several people had apparently been assigned the same seats, and weren't taking it well. Tension in the cabin was high.

The doors finally closed and we taxied to the runway, only to sit for another full hour with no explanation from the crew. I couldn't help but think this gave a whole new meaning to the term "pressurized cabin." Mercifully, we did finally take off, and that's when I met one of my QBQ heroes.

Bonita was a flight attendant. When I first saw her, she

prance 활보하다 **aisle** 복도, 통로 **armload** 한 아름 **one of those** 그런 류의 **draped** 늘어지는 **hold up** 억류하다 **sashay** (구어체로) 경쾌하게 걷다 **overbook** 초과예약하다

. . .

We held you up for an hour, but give me five bucks anyway. '우리는 한 시간 동안 당신을 잡아둘 거예요, 어쨌든 5달러 내놓으세요' 헤드폰 대여비를 받는 다른 항공사를 빗대어 농담 한 것이다.

Well, what ever you do, don't drug test me! '음, 뭘 하셔도 좋은데요, 비행기는 태우지 마세요' drug test는 일반적으로 마약류 검사를 의미하지만 '약 먹고 이렇게 기분이 좋은 것은(잘 하는 것은) 아니에요' 라는 뜻이다. 즉, '날 너무 칭찬하지 마세요' 혹은 '비행기 태우지 마세요' 의 의미로 구어체 상에서 사용된다.

We get high on life. '우리는 삶에서 기쁨을 얻는다' high는 주로 get과 사용되어 get high '기분이 좋다, 즐겁다' 의 의미이다. 하지만 마약에 취하는 것을 의미할 수도 있기 때문에 상황에 따라 주의해 사용해야 한다. 예를 들어 'Do you get high?' 라고 하면 '마약을 하십니까?' 라는 의미가 될 수 있다.

was prancing down the aisle with an armload of headphones, smiling broadly and having great fun. Also, it was the week before Christmas and she was wearing one of those red-and-white Santa Claus caps, which draped down her shoulder and off to one side.

As she handed out the headphones, she wasn't saying, "We held you up for an hour but give me five bucks anyway!" She was offering them at no charge. I watched her turn to a young man and say, "I'm sure you'll enjoy our sports programming, Sir. Here are some headphones!" And to a woman, "I notice you're traveling alone, Ma'am, would you like a friend?"

When she got to me, I stopped her and said, "You know, Bonita, I really appreciate your attitude!" As she sashayed away with that big smile on her face and the Santa Claus cap on her head, she said, "Well, whatever you do, don't drug test me!"

I didn't need to test her. I already knew she was high on life. And that's one of the great things that happens when we make better choices: We get high on life. It's not about "us" versus "them," or "Why did they overbook the plane?" or "Who dropped the ball?" The better question is, "What can I do right now to make a difference?"

With one simple choice, making the best of a bad

one choice at a time '한번에 하나의 선택만'

• • •

What's your boss like?
My boss is one of those quiet persons.
사장님은 어떤 분이세요?
우리 사장님은 좀 조용하신 편이에요.

situation, Bonita made a difference for me and every other person on that flight. That's how personal accountability changes the world: one choice at a time.

ownership 주인의식, 소유권 **illustrate** (예를 들어)설명하다 **static** 잡음
badmouth 깎아내리다, 헐뜯다 **associate** 동료 **affix** (허물, 책임 등을)지우다

· · ·

waited for the blame to roll '비난이 거침없이 나오는 것을 기다렸다' 여기
서 roll은 '(말이) 거침없이 나오다' 라는 뜻으로 쓰였다.

· · ·

Have you made that commitment?
No, I don't think so.
그런 (책임 있는)일을 해본 적 있으세요?
아뇨, 없는 것 같아요.

Chapter Eighteen

Ownership

People frequently talk about a need for "ownership" in our organizations. This story illustrates what they mean:

I was having a problem with static in my phone line, so I contacted our phone company to request a service call. A repairman showed up, worked hard on it and left. But the static came back the next day. A second repairman came and worked on it some more but the problem returned. When the third guy came, I described the problem, paused and waited for the blame to roll. I fully expected him to badmouth his associates, but he didn't. Instead, he said something very powerful: "Mr. Miller, I can't explain it, but I sure can apologize for it!" Ownership: "A commitment of the head, heart and hands to fix the problem and never again affix the blame." Have you made that commitment?

bald eagle 대머리 독수리   **soar** 높이 치솟다   **giraffe** 기린   **cheetah** 치타
appreciate 감사하다

• • •

How ridiculous. ‘참 어리석군’
A teammate is someone who can look right through you and still enjoy the view. ‘팀원이란 바로 당신의 시각을 통해서 모든걸 바라보며 그것을 즐기는 사람이다’

Chapter Nineteen

The Foundation of Teamwork

Would you watch a bald eagle soar and say, "I wish he could swim the seas like a dolphin?" Would you look at a dolphin and hope it someday might reach the heavens like a giraffe? Would you think, "Why can't the lion run as fast as the cheetah?" No, of course not. How ridiculous.

Are you on teams with people who are different from you?

"A teammate is someone who can look right through you and still enjoy the view." Let's appreciate people's gifts and strengths just as they are. That's the foundation of teamwork.

miss the mark 핵심을 놓치다, 빠뜨리다 **set standard** 기준(과표)을 설정하다
define consequence 목표를 정의하다

• • •

Andy obviously missed the mark of the meeting.
Yea. I could hear that he was out of the topic at the meeting.
앤디는 분명히 회의의 핵심을 이해하지 못했어.
네. 회의에서도 계속 주제에서 벗어난 이야기만 하더군요.

Chapter Twenty

Making Accountability Personal: All QBQs Contain an "I"

Right after I had spoken on personal accountability and the QBQ, the CEO of the company got up to say a few words. After a few comments to the hundreds of people before him, he pressed a button that projected this message on a huge screen behind him:

"Personal accountability begins with YOU!"

I know what he was trying to say, but he missed the mark. Personal accountability does NOT begin with you. It begins with me. That's why it's called personal accountability. It is not about you or I holding each other accountable, as a manager does in setting standards, defining consequences, helping set goals and then holding

have control over ~를 통제(제어)하다

· · ·

Accountability groups are great tools. '책임 있는 집단은 그 자체가 대단
한 수단이다' 전반적으로 이 책에서 사용되는 'tool' 은 목적을 위한, 혹은 그
자체가 목적인 것(수단)을 의미한다.

people accountable for their performance. Nor is it a group thing, where people get together, make public professions of commitment, then come back a week or a month later to discuss what did or did not happen.

Personal accountability is about each of us holding ourselves accountable for our own thinking and behaviors and the results they produce.

This is why the second QBQ guideline is: All QBQs contain an "I," not "they," "them," "we" or "you." Questions that contain an "I" turn our focus away from other people and circumstances and put it back on ourselves, where it can do the most good. We can't change other people. We often can't control circumstances and events. The only things we have any real control over are our own thoughts and actions. Asking questions that focus our efforts and energy on what we can do makes us significantly more effective, not to mention happier and less frustrated.

Accountability groups are great tools. Managers and executives do need to define and communicate standards, but the power of personal accountability comes from questions that begin with "What" or "How" and contain an "I."

I bet… 확실히 ~이다 **material** 재료, 원료(여기서는 책이라는 의미) **fix** 고치
다(사람을 목적어로 사용하는 경우는 드묾) **nonprofit** 비영리 **roundtable dis-**
cussion 원탁회의(직위에 관계없이 평등한 발언기회가 주어지는 회의)

• • •

I bet we'll have to lay off some workers this year.
Well. I'm sure someone will raise an objection.
단언하건대 올해는 직원 몇 명을 정리해고 해야 할거야.
글쎄요. 누군가 반대할걸요.

Chapter Twenty One

I Can Only Change Me

Who is the only person I can change? Right—myself. I bet you've known that for a long time. So basic. So fundamental. Here's another question for you: As you've been reading this material, who have you been picturing, thinking, "I wish they could hear this, because they need it?!" It happens all the time. We say, "I can only change me," but then when asked, "Who have you been thinking needs the QBQ?" we say "They do!"

Have you tried to "fix" anybody lately? We all do it. Some of us don't think we're trying to change people, even when we are. A director of a nonprofit said to his four team members in a roundtable discussion, "Really, I'm not trying to change my assistant. I'm not! I just think she should set more long—term goals for herself." Translation:

cautiously 조심스럽게 **deal with** ~을 다루다, 처리하다 **stick in my mind** 마음에 걸리다 **as a result of** ~의 결과로서

· · ·

I want her to be what I want her to be. ‘난 그녀가 내가 원하는 대로 되길 원해’
She went on to explain. ‘그녀는 설명을 계속했다’ go on은 ‘계속 진행하다’ 라는 뜻이다.
put the whole team through training ‘전체 팀에게 훈련과정을 거치게 하다’

· · ·

Will more students attend college as a result of the tax breaks?
Well, I think it's a toss up.
세금감면으로 더 많은 학생들이 학교에 들어올까?
글쎄요. 가능성은 반반일 겁니다.

toss up은 동전 던지기에 의한 결정이라는 뜻으로 50:50의 가능성을 말한다.

"I want her to be what I want her to be."

Others know they're doing it but don't want to admit it. I was talking with a training manager, making final arrangements for delivering a QBQ program for her organization. She said, "Do you want to know why the VP is investing in this program?"

"Sure," I said, cautiously, wondering where this was leading.

"He wants to fix Ed."

Fix Ed?

Ed, she went on to explain, was a supervisor who was struggling in his role. But instead of taking responsibility and dealing with the situation in a direct and honest way, the VP was going to put the whole team through training. "Fix Ed." Those words have always stuck in my mind.

Still others think it's their job to change people. I was visiting with a man in his late twenties who actually said, "I believe it's my job to change people—I'm a manager!" Sorry. Managers don't change people. They can coach, counsel, teach and guide, but no one changes another person. Change only comes from the inside as a result of decisions made by the individual.

This is a hard lesson to learn, and even when we say we "get it," there's a big difference between understanding the

frequently 자주　**pop machine** 자동 판매기　**breakroom** 휴게실　**trick question** 함정이 있는 질문　**mold** 틀에 넣어 만든 것, 주형

· · ·

honestly examining the reality of our thoughts and actions. ‘우리의 생각과 행동의 실제를 정직하게 살펴보는’
Our minds simple don't go there. ‘우리에 생각은 거기에 가지 않는다’ 즉, 우리의 마음에 와 닿지 않는다는 의미이다.
It's based on the truth ‘사실에 기반해서’

idea, "Yes, I can only change myself!" and honestly ex-amining the reality of our thoughts and actions.

Frequently I'll ask a group, "What's the one thing you would change to improve the effectiveness of your organization?" Usually they come out with a list of "**P**s" : **P**roducts, **P**romotions, **P**olicies, **P**rocesses, **P**rocedures, **P**ricing and **P**eople. More people, fewer people, different people. One guy said "Pepsi."(Yes, Pepsi.) "If only we'd switch the pop machine in the breakroom from Coke to Pepsi."

People's minds fill with all kinds of ideas when asked what they would change to improve things. But guess what nobody ever says? Me! "I would change me to make our organization run more effectively." Someone once suggested it was a trick question but I don't think it is. Read it again. Our minds simply don't go there. Our thoughts almost always focus else where first. Asking questions that begin with "What" or "How" and contain an "I" brings our focus back to our selves.

How much better things would be if we all tried to mold and shape our own thoughts and actions rather than those of others. The bottom line is that the QBQ works because it's based on the truth, "I can only change me."

middle manager 중간 관리자 **class ring and yearbook** 학교(졸업이나 축하
용)반지와 졸업앨범 **branch manager** 지점장 **relieve** 안도하다 **get along**
~와 친한 관계를 유지하다 **cooperate** 협력하다 **nail** 못 박히다, 고정시키다

· · ·

I was relieved to be out of the hospital.
Congratulations. But now it's time to take care yourself.
병원에서 퇴원하게 되어서 마음이 놓여요.
축하하네. 그러나 이제부터 자기관리를 잘 해야 하네.

Chapter Twenty Two

"He didn't, I did"

After a presentation, a middle manager at Jostens (the class ring and yearbook company) came up and told me that the idea, "I can only change me," had really touched her. "When I was a branch manager," she explained, "there was a guy reporting to me who I just couldn't seem to manage. We didn't work well together at all. When he transferred to another location across the country, I was relieved."

"A couple of years passed and we found ourselves in the same office with me as his supervisor again! But this time things were different," she said. "We were getting along, communicating well and cooperating on projects. At one point I asked myself, 'When did he change?' but then I realized he didn't change, I had!"

"How did you change?" I asked. Her response nailed it

Her response nailed it right on my head. '그녀에 대답은 내 머리에 각인 되었다'

right on the head:

"I stopped trying to change him."

senior management retreat 최고 경영자 과정 **flip chart** 강연 등에서 발표를 위해 넘기면서 사용하는 큰 종이의 묶음 **stone tablet** 돌로 만든 패 (여기서는 참석했음을 증명하기 위해서 나누어주는 증서나 회의의 내용을 정리해서 나누어주는 브로서 등을 의미) **transform into** ～으로 변형(변모)시키다 **laminated** 얇게 여러 층으로 겹쳐진 **stuff in** ～에 쑤셔 넣다 **huddle** (사람들이) 모이다, 붐비다 **whisper** 속삭이다 **spot** 발견하다, 분별하다 **gap** (갈라진)틈, 구멍, 부족 **integrity** 고결, 완전한 상태, 흠 없음

· · ·

Up to the mountaintop go the executives for a senior management retreat. '산 정상에서 열린 최고 경영자 과정에 여러 경영진이 참가했다'

126

Chapter Twenty Three

"When will others walk their talk?"

Up to the mountaintop go the executives for a senior management retreat. For three days they debate the critical issues, filling flip charts with brightly colored ink. Finally, "mission, vision and values" in hand, they return to the valley below where the people wait to receive the stone tablets, which have been magically transformed into little laminated pocket cards for men to sit on and women to stuff in their briefcases.

Not long after, people huddle near a water cooler, pull out their cards and whisper, "Well, I'll practice these values when they do!"

Careful. The easiest thing to spot is gaps of integrity in others:

The manager who says, "I'm here to help you reach your

dress someone down ~을 꾸짖다, 비난하다 **empower** ~에게 권한을 부여
하다 **the last one budgeted** 예산에 마지막으로 책정되는 **the first one cut**
첫 번째로 삭감되는 **in accordance with** ~의 규칙에 따라서 **espouse** 신봉
하다, 지지하다 **walk one's talk** ~의 말을 실천하다(=walk the walk, talk the
talk)

• • •

The easiest thing to spot is gaps of integrity in others. '가장 쉽게 눈에
띄는 것은 다른 사람들의 빈틈이다'

before you do anything substantial, check with me first. '무엇인가 실제
로 행하기 전에 나에게 우선 상의해주세요' check with me는 '나에게 확인을
받아라, 상의하라' 는 의미로 다소 명령의 뉘앙스가 있는 표현이다.

Being what I say I am by acting in accordance with my words. '내 입에
서 흘러나온 나와 실제의 내가 일치하는 것이다'

• • •

Let's see if he can walk the walk.
But I'm not so sure about his words.
그 사람이 자신의 말처럼 잘하는지 봅시다.
근데 전 그분 말씀에 대해 확신이 안 서요.

128

personal goals" and then dresses people down in front of others.

The executive who says, "You are all empowered. It's our new program!" and then adds, "But before you do anything substantial, check with me first."

The teammate who says, "I appreciate my colleagues just the way they are... but if they'd only be a bit more like me."

The organization that proudly declares on the lobby wall its guiding value, "People are our greatest asset!" yet the training dollar is the last one budgeted and the first one cut.

The definition of integrity is this:

"Being what I say I am by acting in accordance with my words."

QBQ thinking leads to integrity because integrity begins with me—not others—asking the question, "How can I practice the principles I espouse?"

Instead of asking, "When will others walk their talk?" let's walk our own talk first.

match 부합하다, 같다 **harsh** 거친, 가혹한

• • •

Sound harsh?

No. I think It sound reasonable.

좀 심했나요?

아뇨. 전 적절했다고 생각해요.

Chapter Twenty Four

An Integrity Test

Here's an integrity test for anyone who's part of an organization: Does what we say about our organization while we're at work match what we say at home? If it's positive at work and negative a few hours later at home, we have a choice to make. Here's an idea we should all consider:

Believe or leave.

Sound harsh? Maybe. But if the organization is no longer a vehicle to help us reach our life goals, why would we stay?

Answering that question honestly is part of practicing personal accountability.

tempting 하고 싶은 **firm believer** 신봉자 **end up** 결국, 마침내 **substitute**
～와 바꾸다, 대체하다 **excuse** 변명, 구실 **get the job done** 일을 끝마치다

· · ·

We can hide behind the team with thoughts—which became excuse
'우리는 변명이 되는 생각들로 팀 뒤에 숨을 수 있다'

Chapter Twenty Five

The Power of One

One of the most tempting questions to ask when we first learn the QBQ is, "What can we do?" The problem is, "we" don't change. Teams, departments and organizations don't change. People change, one at a time, through their own choices. I'm a firm believer in the team concept, but if we're not careful, we can end up substituting the language of teams ("we" and "us") for the language of personal accountability. We can hide behind the team with thoughts—which become excuses—such as:

"The team didn't meet the deadline."

"The team wasn't given enough resources."

"The team didn't get the job done."

"The team didn't have a clear mission."

와, 정말 수고 했어요.

The power of one 한 명의 힘

· · ·

I had a lot of job, but I finally got it all done.
Wow! You got a really good job.
일이 많았지만 결국 다 끝냈습니다.
와, 정말 수고 했어요.

Personal accountability is not about changing others. It's about making a difference by changing ourselves. Personal accountability. The power of one.

Serenity 평정, 고요함 **a QBQ twist** QBQ식 말 돌림 **God grant me…** (기
도문에서) 신이여 ~함을 허락하소서

Chapter Twenty Six

A QBQ Twist

You may already be familiar with the Serenity Prayer:

"God grant me the serenity to accept the things I cannot change, the courage to change the things I can, and the wisdom to know the difference.

Here's a QBQ twist for all of us:

"God grant me the serenity to accept the people I cannot change, the courage to change the one I can, and the wisdom to know... it's me!"

tremendous 많은, 엄청난 **make a fuss** 소란(야단법석)을 피우다 **sports figure** 유명 스포츠맨 **get out of the line** 앞으로 나서다 **realization** 사실이라고 생각함(깨달음), 현실화 **emulate** 흉내내다, 모방하다

• • •

Will the real role models please stand up! '진짜 역할 모델들이여 일어나라' **shame on them.** '부끄러운 줄 알아라' 구두상으로 사용되는 표현으로 shame on은 '~을 극구 비난하다, 공격하다' 의 의미이다.
It's humbling realization at times. '그건 우리 시대의 비천한 현실이다' **role model** 미국의 신입 사원들은 상사 중에서 Role model을 정하여 따르는 것이 성공의 지름길이라 믿는다.

138

Chapter Twenty Seven

Will the Real Role Models Please Stand Up!

We make a tremendous fuss when a Hollywood star, sports figure, pop singer or politician gets out of line. Shame on them, we say, for being such a bad role model for the children. But in reality, no public figure is a role model for our kids. That' s our job—yours and mine. It's a humbling realization at times but it's the truth.

It's equally true for all of us. No matter what our role, someone is watching and emulating our behavior.

Modeling is the most powerful of all teachers.

Who's watching you?

go through ~의 과정을 마치다 **merger** 합병하다 **afterward** 후에, 나중에 **gripe** 불평하다 **parent company** 모회사(=mother company) **hamper** 방해하다, 구속하다 **one hour or so** 한 시간 정도, 가량 **slip out** 몰래(빠져)나가다 (여기서는 '말이 잘못 나오다'의 의미) **figure out** 이해하다 **head out** ~로 향하다

• • •

I figured out why my boss is mad at me!
So what was that?
사장님이 나에게 화가 난 이유를 알아냈어.
그 이유가 뭐였는데?

Chapter Twenty Eight

Practicing Personal Accountability: All QBQs Focus on Action

A corporation that had just gone through a major merger held a QBQ session. Afterward, a middle manager came up and shared this story with me. He had come into our morning program griping and complaining (his words) about a problem with the new parent company head-quarters in New Jersey that was seriously hampering his field operations. After an hour or so of the QBQ, he began to think differently. He slipped out and called his travel agent to book a ticket for the next day back to the East Coast. He had figured out how to solve the problem.

What a great example of the practice of personal accountability. First, he chose to stop complaining and ask a better question like, "What can I do?" And when the better answer came— "You know what? I could head out

ultimate goal 궁극적(최종) 목표 **cave people** 동굴에 사는 사람, 즉 우물 안 개구리 **end up with** ~로 끝나다 **discipline** 훈련하다 **take action** 행동(조치)을 취하다

· · ·

You know what··· 구두상으로 상대의 주의(attention)를 요구할 때 사용된다. Listen!이나 Look!도 마찬가지다.

· · ·

Alice decided to take action against the unfair tax law.
She filled a lawsuit against the government.
앨리스는 그 부당한 세법에 대해 행동을 취하기로 결심했어.
정부를 상대로 소송을 제기했지.

there, sit down with them and figure this thing out" —he did it. He picked up the phone and made the call.

It's so simple, but the ultimate goal of the QBQ is action!

Our third guideline is: All QBQs focus on action. To make a QBQ action—focused, we add verbs such as "do," "make," "achieve" and "build" to questions that start with "What" or "How" and contain an "I."

Now, if that's all we did, a QBQ might sound something like, "What I do?" or "How I build?" So to avoid sounding like cave people, we add another word or two such as "can" or "will" and "now" or "today," and end up with excellent—sounding questions like, "What can I do right now?" and "How will I make a difference today?"

If we don't ask what we can do or make or achieve or build, then we won't do or make or achieve or build. It's just that simple. Only through action is anything accomplished.

The practice of personal accountability: We discipline our thoughts. We ask better questions. We take action.

senior leader 고위층 지도자, 간부 **take risk** 위험을 감수하다 **eliminate** 제거하다, 삭제하다 **lack of initiative** 독창성의 부족 **alternative** 양자택일
inaction 게으름

• • •

our lack of initiative today may guarantee out lack of employment tomorrow. '독창성의 부족으로 인해 실직하게 될지도 모른다'

Chapter Twenty Nine

The Risk of Doing Nothing

A senior leader of a financial institution told me, "Sometimes people say to me, 'I don't want to take risks.' I tell them, 'You and I had better take risks, because there are about a dozen people at their computers right now in this building trying to eliminate our jobs!'" What was he really saying? None of us has guaranteed job security, and our lack of initiative today may guarantee our lack of employment tomorrow. Taking action may seem risky, but doing nothing is a bigger risk!

Even though there are risks involved in taking action, the alternative, inaction, is almost never the better choice:

• Action, even when it leads to mistakes, brings learning

stagnation 정체, 부진 **atrophy** 퇴화, 쇠약 **at best** 잘해야, 기껏해야
confidence 신임, 자신감, 확신

• • •

It's better to be one who is told to wait than one who waits to be told.
'알 때까지 기다리는 사람보다는 알고 기다리는 사람이 낫다'

• • •

At best, July and I dated a few times.
Really? But she told me she is in love with you.
줄리와 나는 그냥 몇 번 데이트 했을 뿐이야.
그래? 근데 그녀는 너를 사랑한다고 말하던걸?

146

and growth. Inaction brings stagnation and atrophy.

- Action leads us toward solutions. Inaction at best does nothing and holds us in the past.
- Action requires courage. Inaction often indicates fear.
- Action builds confidence; inaction, doubt.

A friend said, "It's better to be one who is told to wait, than one who waits to be told."

Decide what to do. Then take action.

in a hurry 다급한, (바빠서)허둥대는 **plunk down** 쿵 하고 내려놓다, (돈을)지불하다 **standard procedure** 표준 처리방침 **break the hundred** 100달러를 깨다, 잔돈으로 바꾸다 **pneumatic tube** 기송관(관을 통해 공기압으로 운반하는 장치) **not to mention** 말할 것도 없이, 당연히

• • •

Home Depot 미국에서 가정, 사무용 건설 자재를 전문적으로 판매하는 매장. 미국인들은 집을 손수 가꾸거나 수리하는 문화가 일반화되어 있기 때문에 모든 관련된 재료들을 직접 구매하기도 한다.

Chapter Thirty

"Thanks for Shopping at the Home Depot!"

One morning a few weeks into Judy's new job as a cashier at Home Depot, a young man came through her line, obviously in a hurry. He quickly plunked down a few items and a hundred-dollar bill, but the total came to only two dollars and eighty-nine cents. "Do you have anything smaller?" Judy asked. "No, I'm sorry, I don't," he said. At that moment, Judy had a choice to make.

Since she'd just opened up for the day, she only had forty dollars in her drawer. Standard procedure said that to break the hundred, she'd need to put it in a pneumatic tube and send it up to the office. But Judy thought that would take more time than her customer seemed to have—not to mention the other customers in line behind him.

So here's what she did: She handed the young man back

tear off 찢어버리다   **somewhat stunned** 약간 놀라서   **take off** 구어상에서 '(급히) 자리를 뜨다, 나가다'   **get straight** 똑바로(있는 그대로) 말하다, 오해를 바로잡다   **abruptly** 불쑥, 갑자기

· · ·

As far as Judy was concerned, that was the end of it. '그녀에게 있어서 그 일은 끝난 일이었다'

endorse '배서하다' 미국의 경우 수표 사용이 일반화되어 있다. 수취인의 기명(endorsement)이 없으면 입금(deposit)이 불가능하다.

Yes, I guess I did. '네, 그랬던 것 같아요' 구두상에서 I believe, think, guess 는 '믿다, 생각하다, 추측하다' 라는 의미보다는 확신이 없을 때 사용된다. 즉, '~인 것 같아요, ~일 거예요' 등으로 해석한다.

· · ·

Mr. Silver. Is it OK if I take off now?
Sure you may go. Have a good one.
실버 씨. 지금 퇴근해도 되나요?
물론, 가도 좋네. 좋은 하루 보내게.

his bill, reached down for her purse, took out the two-eighty-nine, put it in the register and tore off the receipt. She turned to her customer with a smile and said, "Thanks for shopping at the Home Depot!"

The man stood there a few moments before he figured out what she'd done. Finally, somewhat stunned, he thanked her several times and took off. As far as Judy was concerned, that was the end of it.

Two days later, her supervisor, looking both confused and amused, approached her holding an envelope.

"Judy, I need to get this straight," he said. "Did you actually buy the merchandise for one of our customers the other day?"

She had to think. "Yes, I guess I did."

"Well, he's sent you a tip," he said, "and as a Home Depot employee, I'm sure you know you can't accept tips."

"I don't want a tip," she said, then abruptly added, "How much?"

"He wrote you a check for fifty dollars."

"Wow! How about if I endorse it and put it in the pizza fund so we can all share it?" she asked.

"OK," he said. "We can do that."

So the money went into the pizza fund and no one thought any more of it.

Sr. senior, 혹은 1세 **constructor** 건설자, 건설회사 **stuff** 어떤 사물(여기서는 건축자재) **prospective** 예상된, 기대되는 **you folks** 당신 사람들(여기서는 네 회사 사람들) **be willing to** 기꺼이(자발적으로) ∼하다 **tight spot** 난처한 입장 **line up** 줄 서 있다 **stressed out** 스트레스로 지친

· · ·

Isn't that something? '대단하지 않나요?' something은 사람이나 대상을 격상시키는 의미도 있다.

Never let it be said one person can't have an impact. '결코 한 개인이 강한 영향력을 발휘할 수 없다고 말하지 말아라'

She didn't get stressed out. '그녀는 스트레스를 받지 않았다'

She kept her cool. '그녀는 냉정함을 유지했다'

Judy, I've got to know. '주디, 난 알아야겠어요'

· · ·

You look really stressed out.

I know but I'm still behind my work.

너무 지쳐 보여!

알아. 하지만 아직 할 일이 많이 남아 있어.

The next day, though, the young man showed up in her line again. This time, he had with him his father, Bob Johnson Sr., owner of Johnson Construction Company. Question: What do contractors need? Answer: Stuff! And the better answer from Judy's perspective: Stuff from the Home Depot.

The elder Mr. Johnson said to Judy, "I want you to know that because of what you did to serve my son the other day, we've decided to start getting everything we need from you folks!"

Isn't that something? Never let it be said one person c-an' t have an impact, especially if he or she is willing to take risks. Remember, Judy was in kind of a tight spot. The young man was in a hurry, people were lined up behind him and standard procedure said she'd have to make them all wait while she got change. But she didn't get stressed out, thinking, "Why is this happening to me?" or just say, "Sorry, it's sour policy" and make them wait. She kept her cool and decided to take action and serve her customer. That's QBQ service, and it's worth the risk.

But the story's not quite over yet. Right after the elder Mr. Johnson spoke, the younger leaned over the counter and whispered to Judy,

"Judy, I've got to know."

How much higher would you have gone? '얼마나 더 높은 액수까지 내줄 수 있었겠어요?' 이 문장은 다양하게 해석될 수 있다. 즉, '내가 그만큼 신뢰가 갔나요?', '절 위해 얼마나 감수할 수 있으세요?' 또한 경우에 따라 호감을 표시하는 것으로 볼 수도 있다.

"You've got to know what?" she whispered back.

"The day you bought my merchandise... how much higher would you have gone?!"

wrestle with ～와 씨름하다 **peer** 동료, (나이, 지위 능력 등이)비슷한 사람
confidently 확신을 갖고, 자신 있게

· · ·

he jumped up in the back row and yelled. '그는 뒷줄에서 벌떡 일어나 소
리쳤다'

· · ·

Are you going to install an alarm system in your new house?
You bet!
너희 새 집에 경보시스템을 장착할거니?
물론이지!

you bet은 '당연하지', '날 믿어' 라고 해석되며 absolutely와 같은 의미이다.

Chapter Thirty One

Leaders at All Levels

Are you a leader? Many people wrestle with this question. "Am I a leader or is my manager the leader? Is the company president the leader? The vice president of my division?" Or they think, "Maybe the leader is my peer who was granted the title of 'Team Leader.' "

I met one man though, who had no question about it at all. I had just asked a group, "Are you a leader?" when he jumped up in the back row and yelled, "I'm a leader, John. You bet—I am a leader!"

I asked him, "What's your name, Sir?" and he said, "Jim Leader." True story. Jim Leader. I checked his license to be sure. James D. Leader, 33 years old. You know what that means? For at least 31 years now he's been able to say confidently not only, "I'm a leader" but also, "I'm a

tenure 재직기간('종신 재직권'을 의미하기도 함) **boastfully** 자랑하며, 자화자찬의 **loyalty** 충실함 **admirable quality** 존경할 만한 가치 **equate with** ~와 같다고 여기다 **merely** 단지, 다만 **moment-to-moment** 매 순간 **temp worker** 임시직 노동자

. . .

don't get me wrong. '오해하지 마세요'

. . .

Don't equate criticism with blame.
But it sounds like blame not criticism.
비평을 비난이라고 생각하지 마세요.
그러나 비평이 아닌 비난으로 들리는데요?

158

born Leader!"

For most of us though, it's not that simple. Too often, we think leadership is about title, position, the number of people or dollars we manage or tenure. I find the tenure thing especially funny. When I hear someone say boastfully, "I've been here over a dozen years!" I can just imagine someone else in that organization saying, "Yeah, and that may be your problem!"

Don't get me wrong, loyalty is an admirable quality. But the number of years one has been around does not automatically equate with being a good leader, any more than does merely having the title of manager or vice president. And certainly the things we acquire — fine cars, nice homes — are not measures of our leadership ability.

Leadership, more than anything else, is about the way we think. It's a moment-to-moment disciplining of our thoughts. It's about practicing personal accountability and choosing to make a positive contribution, no matter what our role or "level." A receptionist, an engineer, a sales per-son, a temp worker, a cashier: They all can be leaders. Judy certainly was. Parents? Absolutely. Parenting may be the most important leadership role there is. Are you a friend, little league coach, volunteer, someone who has

have influence with ~을 움직이는 힘이 있다 **hold true** 유효하다

• • •

If we think like leader, we are leaders.
'우리가 리더처럼 생각한다면 우리도 리더이다'

influence with others at work? The same principle holds true: If we think like leaders, we are leaders.

So I'll ask you again. Are you a leader? Think about it.

recognition 인정, 인식

. . .

It's time we gave her some recognition. ‘이제는 그녀를 알아줘야 할 때이다’
Wait a minute, Jake, who works for whom here anyway? “잠깐만 제이
크, 근데 지금 누가 누구를 위해서 일하는 거지?”

Chapter Thirty Two

The Cornerstone of Leadership

Do you remember Jacob Miller from Chapter One? He was our QBQ hero from the Rock Bottom restaurant who sent his manager to get me a Diet Coke. Well, Jacob was not the only hero in that story. His manager was one, too. And it's time we gave her some recognition.

Think about this: Jacob ran to her and said, "Hey, would you get this guy a Diet Coke?" What did she say? "Yes!" But more importantly, what didn't she say? She didn't come back with one of these responses:

"Wait a minute Jake, who works for whom here anyway?"

"Well, I don't know, what have you done for me lately?"

"Remember when you dropped the ball?"

performance review 인사고과 **hitting your number** 숫자에 도달하다, (만족할 만한)성과에 도달하다 **servant leadership** 봉사나 희생을 통한 리더십 **humble spirit** 겸허한 마음(정신) **cornerstone** 주춧돌, 초석

· · ·

Humility is the cornerstone of leadership. '겸손은 리더십의 초석이다'

"If I do this for you, what will you do for me?"

Or how about this one: "Let me check your performance review and see if you're hitting your numbers. If you are, I may just help you."

She could have asked questions like these, but she didn't. Instead, in the moment, she served Jacob as she would any customer—internal or external. She didn't say, "You succeed, then I'll serve you," but rather, "I will serve you so you can succeed."

Not, "I'm the boss, so you're here for me," but, "As a leader, I'm here to help you reach your goals." "Servant leadership" is the QBQ way, and it requires a humble spirit combined with a servant's heart.

Humility is the cornerstone of leadership.

give a talk 강연하다 **studiously** 학문적으로, 열심히 **lost in thought** (생각에)몰두하다 **covering for people** 사람들을 감싸다, 덮어주다 **take on** 맡아서 경영하다 **all by my self** 완전히 홀로 **disservice** 해, 폐, 모진 짓 **step in** ~에 관어하다, 발을 들여놓다 **team's ball** 팀의 책임, 잘못

· · ·

Let me be clear. '확실하게 해 두죠'

· · ·

I can't continue to cover for you because I feel like a liar.
I'm so sorry. It won't be happen again. I promise.
내가 거짓말쟁이처럼 느껴져 이제 더 이상 네 실수를 덮어 줄 수 없어.
정말 미안해. 약속할게. 다시는 그런 일 없을거야.

Chapter Thirty Three

Leaders are Not Problem Solvers

After giving a talk in my home city of Denver, I rode down the hotel elevator with a woman who had attended the session. She studiously reviewed her notes, lost in thought. Before we reached the lobby she looked up at me and spoke: "So what you're saying, John, is I should go back to the office and do other people's work for them?"

"Whoa, where did that come from?" I thought. "I must not have been clear enough about that." Let me be clear now: The QBQ is not about covering for people, taking on their duties and responsibilities or doing it "all by myself." That is not a service to others, it is a disservice to everyone.

When managers step in and close the sale, when project leaders carry the team's ball, when parents clean the ch-

tackle the problem 문제를 다루다

. . .

How else can people learn? '사람들이 그밖에 달리 배울 수 있는 방법이 있
겠는가?'

ild's room—it teaches nothing positive and adds no real value. As my mentor, W. Steven Brown always taught, "Leaders are not problem solvers, but problem givers." They let others tackle the problem, design their own solutions and take action. How else can people learn? How else can leaders serve?

introductory remarks 소개하는 말들　**capture** (마음을)사로잡다　**empty stare** 무관심한(멍한) 시선　**glare** 노려봄, 쏘아봄　**foreboding cloud** 불길한 기운　**sweat** 땀을 흘리다　**eternity later** 한참 후에서야

· · ·

crunch for time '시간을 곱씹다' crunch는 주로 소리가 '아삭하다' 는 표현의 의성어로 사용된다. 여기서는 째각째각 돌아가는 초침의 소리로 표현했다. **death pause** '어색하고 불편한 정적' 특히 비즈니스에서 고객의 냉담한 반응을 표현하기도 한다.

Chapter Thirty Four

A Great List of Lousy Questions

Jim Ryan, president of Carlson Marketing Group, sat behind the desk. He was polite but crunched for time. He had thirty minutes.

After a few introductory remarks, the visitor—younger, without an impressive title and a bit nervous but still hoping to capture his potential client's interest—asked, "Jim, have you ever heard questions like these?" and shared several questions he called "IQs." Then came what's commonly known in sales as a "death pause": A person asks a question and instead of an immediate response gets back an empty stare, sometimes even a glare.

The death pause hung in the room like a heavy, foreboding cloud. The visitor was starting to sweat. An eternity later, Jim smiled and said, "Wow, that's a great list

lousy question 혐오스러운(한심하기 짝이 없는)질문 **piqued**(호기심, 홍미를)돋
우다 **play a role** ~의 역할을 하다 **order out** 주문을 내다 **on time** 정시에
the field 현장 직원들 **instructions** (제품 등의)사용 설명서, 지시

• • •

When will shipping start getting orders out on time? '언제쯤이면 배송
팀에서 정시에 주문을 처리할 수 있을까?

of really lousy questions!"

Yes! The IQs worked. His interest was piqued. And the questions worked because like most people, he'd heard them before. From the guest chair I smiled back, confident a successful relationship had begun.

Now let's look at our own list of lousy questions. Each of us plays many different roles in our lives, and each of those roles has its own particular challenges and frustrations. As we read the following list of roles with IQs and QBQs, let's think about what IQs we might be asking, and more importantly, what QBQs we could use instead.

Customer service:

"When will shipping start getting orders out on time?"

"Why does the customer expect so much?"

"When will the field do it right the first time?"

"Why don't customers follow the instructions?"

QBQ: "How can I serve them?"

Sales:

"Why are our prices so high?"

"When are we going to be more competitive?"

"Why won't the customer call me back?"

When will they learn to sell the right specs? ‘언제쯤이면 사람들이 성능을 제대로 알고 판매할 수 있을까?’ spec은 보통 구어체 상에서 ‘성능’이나 ‘평가기준’ 등을 의미한다.

Why aren’t they motivated? ‘왜 저 사람들은 동기부여가 안 될까?(의욕적이지 못할까?)

"When will marketing give us better brochures?"

"Why can't manufacturing make what we sell?"

QBQs: "What can I do today to be more effective?"

"How can I add value for my customers?"

Operations or manufacturing:

"Why can't the salespeople stay within our capabilities?"

"When will they learn to sell the right specs?"

QBQ: "How can I better understand the challenges in the field?"

Management:

"Why doesn't the younger generation want to work?"

"When am I going to find good people?"

"Why aren't they motivated?"

"Who made the mistake?"

"Why can't people come in on time?"

QBQs: "How can I be a more effective coach?"

"What can I do to better understand each person on the team?"

front line 최 일선의 현장 **clarify** 명백하게 하다

· · ·

When will the market turn around? '언제 경기가 회복국면으로 돌아올까?'

· · ·

The economy appears to be turning around.
It's a good news to us. Isn't it?

경제가 회복국면에 들어섰어.
그건 우리에게 좋은 소식이죠. 그렇죠?

Executive:

"Who dropped the ball?"

"When are they going to catch the vision?"

"Who will care as much as I do?"

"When will the market turn around?"

QBQs: "How can I be a better leader?"

"What can I do to show I care?"

"How can I communicate better?"

The "Front Line:"

"Why do we have to go through all this change?"

"When is someone going to train me?"

"Why don't I get paid more?"

"Who's going to clarify my job?"

"When is management going to get their act together?"

"Who's going to give us the vision?"

QBQs: "What can I do to be more productive?"

**"How can I adapt to the changing environ-
ment?"**

"What can I do to develop myself?"

sales reps(=sales representative) 세일즈맨, 외판원 **listen to someone** ~의 말
을 따르다 **hang out** ~와(~에서) 어울리다 **open up**(one's mind) 마음을 열
다 **mess** 난잡해진 것

· · ·

when will the salespeople deliver our programs? '언제쯤이면 세일즈맨
들이 우리의 프로그램을 정확히 수행해낼까?'
get through these tough years '이 어려운 시기를 이겨내다'

· · ·

Jack and Jill have been hanging out a lot together. Are they dating?
No they are just friends.
잭과 질이 오랫동안 어울리던데 둘이 사귀니?
아니야. 둘은 그냥 친구사이야.

Marketing:

"When will the salespeople deliver our programs?"

"Why won't the field learn more about our new products?"

QBQs: "What can I do to understand the sales reps' frustrations?"

"How can I learn more about what the customer needs?"

And from the world outside of work ...

Parent:

"When is my child going to listen to me?"

"Why does she hang out with those kids?"

"When will he open up?"

"Who made the mess in here?"

"Why can't you be more like your sister?"

QBQs: "How can I get to know him better?"

"What can I do to improve my parenting skills?"

"How can I simply help her get through these tough years?"

spouse 배우자 **let go** 보내다, 놓아주다

• • •

When are my parents going to get it? '우리 부모님은 언제 그것을 이해하
게 될까?' 여기서 get은 '이해하다' 라는 뜻으로 쓰였다.

Teenager:

"When are my parents going to get it?"

"Why don't they like my friends?"

"Why is my teacher so difficult?"

QBQs: "How can I show more respect to Mom and Dad?"

"What can I do to communicate more effectively?"

"How can I improve my study habits?"

Spouse/Partner:

"Why doesn't he let go of that old issue?"

"When will she appreciate me more?"

"Why don't you start exercising?"

QBQs: "How can I improve myself today?"

"What can I do to help her out?"

Neighbor:

"Why are they so unfriendly?"

QBQ: "How can I be a better friend?"

volunteer 자원봉사자 **set boundary** 기준선(경계)을 정하다 **be up to** ~에 달려 있다

· · ·

What can I do to set better boundaries and just say 'no'. '더 나은 기준 을 정하고 아닌 것은 아니라고 말하기 위해서 무엇을 할 수 있을까?'

· · ·

Let it go your anger.

Yes I know. But I can't stop thinking about it.

화난 거 그만 잊어버려.

나도 알아. 하지만 그 생각을 떨쳐버릴 수가 없어.

Volunteer:

"Why do I have to do everything myself?"

QBQ: "What can I do to set better boundaries and just say 'no' ?"

IQs or QBQs. The choice is up to us. Let's choose wisely, because the questions we ask can make all the difference in the world.

well-established 안정된, 확립된 **underlying** 근원적인, 뒤에 숨어 있는
compliance with ~에 따라, 순응하여 **in alignment with** ~와 일직선상의
(일직선이 되어)

· · ·

There's a difference between the "letter" and the "spirit" of the law.
'법의 정신과 그 구체적인 문안(형식)에는 차이가 있다'

· · ·

Compliance with the law is expected of everyone.
Yea. Then we don't need any prison. Huh?
모든 사람은 법에 따라 살아야 해.
그러게, 그럼 감옥은 필요 없겠다. 그렇지?

Chapter thirty Five

The Spirit of the QBQ

There's a well-established legal principle that says there's a difference between the "letter" and the "spirit" of the law. The letter of the law refers to the specific words used in the law itself. The spirit refers to the underlying concepts and intentions behind the law. The general idea is that compliance with the letter of the law should be in alignment with the spirit of the law. Using the same concept in our case, the letter of the QBQ would be the guidelines.

1. Begin with "What" or "How," (**not** "Why," "When" or "Who").
2. Contain an "I" (**not** "they," "them," "we" or "you").
3. Focus on action.

mention 언급하다 **construct**(문장 등을)만들다 **conflict with** ~와 충돌하다
When the time comes to construct a meaningful question '의미 있는 질
문을 해야 할 때가 오면'

· · ·

The two groups have been in conflict with each other for years.
Yea. They've been lead a cat and dog life.
그 두 그룹은 오랫동안 서로 충돌해왔지.
맞아, 그들은 앙숙으로 살아왔어.

The spirit of the QBQ is personal accountability:

• No more victim thinking, procrastinating or blaming.
• I can only change me.
• Take action!

I mention this because it's possible to construct a question that follows the letter of the QBQ but conflicts with the spirit. Consider these:

"What can I do to make you change?"
"How can I avoid responsibility in this matter?"
"What action can I take right now to do the wrong thing?"
 Or my son's favorite, "Who can I blame today?"

OK, my son's doesn't even follow the letter. The others do, yet they're clearly not QBQs. The principle is this: If a question conflicts with the spirit of the QBQ, it isn't a QBQ.

Playing with QBQs like these can be fun. But when the time comes to construct a meaningful question, remember that the only questions that will help us practice personal accountability are those that follow both the letter and the spirit of the QBQ.

전해나갈 수 있다는 의미이다.

What we learn after we know it all. '다 알고 나서야 배우게 되는 것'
I'm not a finished product. '나는 완성된 상품이 아니다' 계속 변화하고 발
전해나갈 수 있다는 의미이다.

Wisdom

Wisdom: What we learn after we know it all.

I'm not a finished product. Are you?

merely 단지, 다만 **translate into** ~으로 바꾸다, 고치다

• • •

It's all wasted if we're unclear on what learning really is. '우리가 진정
한 배움에 대해 제대로 알지 못한다면 그것은 모두 낭비일 뿐이다'

We Buy Too Many Books

We attend too many seminars. We take too many classes. We buy too many books. We play too many audios in our cars. It's all wasted if we're unclear on what learning really is: Learning is not attending, listening or reading. Nor is it merely gaining knowledge. Learning is really about translating knowing what to do into doing what we know. It's about changing.

If we have not changed we have not learned. What have you learned today?

come upon 우연히 만나다 **blowing around** 사방으로 날리는 **oldest** 장남 (녀) **chase** 뒤쫓다, 추적하다 **gather around** ~의 주위로 모이다 **clutch** 꽉 잡다

• • •

Many hands make light work. '여러 일손이 일을 쉽게 한다' 백지장도 맞 들면 낫다는 우리 속담과 같은 뜻이다.
he rested on one hip, clutched the few papers he had been able to nab. '그는 몇 장의 종이를 가능한 한 꽉 움켜쥔 채 한 쪽 엉덩이로 앉아 쉬었다'

Chapter Thirty Eight

A Final Picture

The Miller family was driving down the highway on a windy Sunday afternoon when we came upon the most amazing scene: In a field off to the side of the road, we saw a man dive from his wheelchair into a sea of newspapers that were blowing around in the Denver wind. He was trying to catch them but the wind was strong and in a moment the field was almost completely covered. From the back of the van, Kristin, our oldest, yelled, "Dad, let's go help that guy!" So we quickly parked and all of us raced out to help. As we chased down papers, hugging them to our chests, I wondered what had happened.

"Many hands make light work," the saying goes, and the job was soon done. As we gathered around the gentleman, he rested on one hip, clutched the few papers he had been

nab 잡다, 움켜쥐다(주로 '범인을 체포하다' 의 의미)   **uselessness** 소용없음, 헛됨   **bundle** 묶음, 다발   **pickup** 짐을 실을 수 있는 작은 트럭

• • •

with one arm shaking almost to the point of uselessness '거의 제 기능을 못할 정도로 떨리는 한 쪽 팔로'
Without really thinking it through first '처음에는 충분히 생각해보지 않고'

able to nab and silently searched for words.

One of the kids asked him, "What happened?" and after struggling back into his wheelchair, with one arm shaking almost to the point of uselessness, he said, "I got home and noticed a whole bundle had disappeared from my pick-up. Driving back this direction, I saw the field covered and I couldn't believe my eyes!"

Without really thinking it through first, I asked, "And you were going to pick them up all by yourself?"

He looked at me as if I didn't get it and said, "I couldn't just leave them. It was my mess."

My mess. My responsibility. What a powerful picture of personal accountability. As we've said throughout this book, personal accountability is not blaming, complaining and putting things off, but instead asking questions like, "What can I do?" and taking action. We've offered guidelines for constructing better questions—all QBQs begin with "What" or "How," contain an "I" and focus on action—suggesting that asking QBQs is the way to start disciplining our thoughts and making better choices.

As we go out now and apply the QBQ in our own lives, let's always remember the real reason we're doing it. We're doing it so we can be more like the people we've read about in this book: Jacob, the server at the Rock Bottom

handicapped 장애가 있는(disabled가 바른 표현이다) **crawl** 기어가다 **em-
body** 구체화하다, 구현하다 **finger-pointing** (부당한)비난, 지탄 **"we-they"
ing** 편 가르기 **far better** 훨씬 더 좋은

• • •

with me standing at the front of the line '나와 함께 앞장서서'
as loudly to you as it does to me '나에게 그러하듯이 당신에게도 크게'
May it serve you well in all you do. '당신이 하는 모든 일에서 그것(QBQ)
이 잘 작동하기를' may가 평서형 문장 맨 앞에 오면 무언가를 기원하는 의미
로 쓰인다. 영화 〈스타워즈〉의 제다이 기사들이 주고 받는 유명한 대사도
may를 사용하고 있다. May the force be with you. '포스가 당신과 함께 하길'

• • •

I'm not going to point the finger at anyone in particular.
because I don't know specifically who did this.
나는 누가 이 짓을 했는지 모릅니다.
따라서 딱히 누구를 손가락질 하진 않을 겁니다.

196

restaurant; Stacey's father, the pilot; Bonita, the flight attendant; Judy, the cashier at the Home Depot; and our "handicapped" friend with the newspapers (his name was Brian) who got down and crawled around in a field because it was "his mess."

None of these people knew about the QBQ, but each embodied its spirit. The rest of us, though, with me standing at the front of the line, need the QBQ. We may not need it every minute of every day, but we need it often enough for it to make a real difference in our lives.

We need the QBQ so our organizations can be places where instead of finger-pointing, procrastinating and "we-they"ing ourselves into the ground, we bring out the best in each other, work together the way teams are supposed to and make great things happen.

It's an exciting vision that I hope speaks as loudly to you as it does to me, because if more people practiced personal accountability, the world would be a far better place.

The QBQ. The Question Behind the Question. May it serve you well in all you do.

Repetition is the motor of learning. ‘학습의 원동력은 반복이다’
What's that again?/I beg your pardon? ‘다시 한번 말해주시겠습니까?’
회의 등에서 사용하는 정중한 표현도 있다. Would you please run that by
me again?

Chapter Thirty Nine

The Motor of Learning

Repetition is the motor of learning.

What' s that again?

Repetition is the motor of learning.

I beg your pardon?

Repetition is ...

OK, I get it!

Great. So now that you've finished the book, read it again.

바보들은 항상 남의 탓만 한다

〈한글 요약문〉

Introduction : 도대체 무슨 일이 벌어진 거지?

오늘날 우리가 직면하는 대부분의 문제는 바로 부족한 책임의식에서 비롯된다. 반대로 우리의 조직과 삶을 개선하기 위한 가장 효과적인 방법은 지금까지의 사고방식을 뒤집어 스스로 책임의식을 불러일으키도록 질문하는 것이다. QBQ(Question Behind the Question)란 모든 개인이 스스로의 책임을 다하도록 돕기 위해 오랫동안 개발되고 다듬어진 효과적인 질문기법을 말한다.

1. 도대체 우리의 책임의식은 어디로 사라진 걸까?

종업원이 매니저에게 '콜라 하나 사다 주세요' 하고 요구할 수 있다니! 이것이야말로 진정한 의미의 권한위임 아닌가! 이 종업원의 행동은 개인적 책임의식과 QBQ의 실체를 잘 보여주는 행동이다. QBQ의 함축적 본질은 발전적인 질문을 통해, 주어진 순간에 더욱 발전적인 선택을 하는 것이다.

2. 더 나은 선택

무엇이 되었든 간에 스스로 선택해야 하는 책임 그리고 그 선택을 할 때 반드시 발전적인 선택을 해야 하는 책임은 바로 우리 자신에게 있다. 이 개념이 바로 QBQ의 토대이다. 어떤 사람들은 무엇이든 '도무지 선택의 여지가 없다' 라고 말하기도 한다. 그리고 '나는…해야만 해!' 또는 '나는 도저히 할 수 없어!' 라는 식의 표현을 자주 사용한다. 그러나 선택의 길은 열려 있다.

3. QBQ! 해답은 질문 속에 있다

무언가에 관해서 처음 반응을 보일 때, 사람들은 대체로 부정적이며 그릇된 질문, 즉 IQ(Incorrect Question)에 기반을 둔 생각이 먼저 튀어나오기 마련이다. QBQ는 그러한 경험에서 비롯된 기법이다. QBQ의 중요한 원리 중의 하나는 '해답은 질문 속에 있다'는 사실이다. 질문을 할 때 '왜?, 언제?, 누가'가 아닌 '무엇?' '어떻게'로 시작하는 질문을 사용해야 한다. 또한 '그들?, 우리?, 당신'이 아닌 '나'를 포함하는 질문을 사용해야 한다. 이것이 발전적인 질문이다. 마지막으로 모든 질문은 행동에 초점을 맞춰야 한다.

4. 제발, 왜냐고 묻지 마라

QBQ의 첫 번째 지침은 바로 이것이다. 모든 QBQ는 '왜?, 언제?, 누가'가 아니라 '무엇' 또는 '어떻게'로 시작해야 한다는 점이다.

"어떻게 하면 지금 내가 하고 있는 일을 더 잘할 수 있을까?"

"현재 상황을 개선하기 위해 내가 무엇을 할 수 있을까?"

"어떻게 하면 내가 다른 사람들을 도울 수 있을까?"

5. 희생양

10년 동안 군인으로 변명 없는 삶을 살았던 사람이 기업으로 옮기면서 스스로를 희생양으로 만드는 질문을 반복하는 자신의 모습을 발견한다. 우리 또한 언제라도 이런 지경에 처할 수 있다는 사실을 잊어서는 안 될 것이다.

6. 왜 이 일이 나에게 일어나는 걸까?

스트레스는 선택의 문제다. 지금 당신 스스로 스트레스를 만들어내고 있는 것은 아닌가? 우리의 삶은 늘 이런 '원치 않는 일' 들로 점철되어 있다. 그러나 분명 스트레스는 선택의 문제다. 어떤 '사건' 이 발생하건 간에 그 대응방식은 우리의 선택에 달려 있기 때문이다. 분노를 표현하거나 두려움을 드러낼 수도 있지만, 감정을 자제하여 침착하게 대응할 수도 있다.

7. 왜 우리는 변화를 감내해야 할까?

만약 당신이 새로운 문제에 직면하여 그에 맞게 상황을 변화시키기 원한다면 새로운 전략이 필요하다. 뿐만 아니라 예기치 않은 상황에 적절히 대응하기 위해서는 다양한 대응방법을 준비해두어야 한다. 변화를 거부하고 한숨과 불평에 사로잡혀 '난 한 번도 이런 식으로 해 본 적인 없는데!' 혹은 '왜 이 모든 변화를 받아들여야 하는 거지?' 와 같은 생각만 하고 있다면, 매우 비극적인 결과가 발생할 수도 있다.

8. 왜 의사소통이 어려울까?

의사소통이란, 상대방에게 나를 이해시키는 것이 전부가 아니다. 그것 못지않게 중요한 것은 내가 상대방을 이해하는 것이다. QBQ로 표현하자면 이런 질문이 될 수 있겠다. '어떻게 하면 내가 당신을 더 잘 이해할 수 있을까?'

9. '언제?' 라고 묻지 마라

'언제?'를 들먹이는 것은, 다음 차례나 기회가 올 때까지 마냥 기다리거나 행동을 보류할 수밖에 없다는 의미이다. 따라서 '언제'로 시작하는 질문은 그 질문을 던진 당사자의 태만을 말해 줄 뿐이다. '언제?'라는 질문 대신 다음과 같은 발전적인 질문을 던져야 한다. '지금 내가 제시할 수 있는 해결책에는 어떤 것이 있는가?'

10. 태만, 실패의 친구

작은 문제가 있다면, 작은 상태일 때 빨리 해결하는 습관을 들여야 한다. 호미로 막을 수 있는 건 호미로 막는 게 훨씬 쉽고 효율적이다.

11. 언제 더 나은 것을 가질 수 있을까?

현재 가지지 못한 것에 미련을 가지고 집착하는 것은 시간 낭비, 에너지 낭비일 뿐이다. 정말로 남다르고 탁월한 결과를 얻고 싶다면, 현실 속에서 성공적인 결과를 얻는 데 집중해야 한다.

12. 언제 새로운 아이디어를 습득할 수 있나?

문제는 새로운 아이디어가 부족한 게 아니라, '기존'의 아이디어가 여전히 효과적이란 사실을 이해하지 못하는 데 있다. 우리에게 필요한 것은 새로운 정보가 아니다. 정말로 필요한 것은, 평소에 개인적인 책임의식과 같은 '기본'을 충실히 이행하는 것이다. "내가 이미 알고 있는 것을 어떻게 적용할까?" 하고 묻는 편이 훨씬 바람직하다.

13. '누가?' 라고 묻지 말자

비난이란 조직의 규모와는 아무런 상관이 없다. 아주 작은 집단에서 거대 기업에 이르기까지, 그리고 말단 신입사원에서 최고 경영진에 이르기까지, 비난은 전염병처럼 퍼져 있으며 비난 바이러스의 면역체를 가진 사람은 아무도 없다. 비난과 '누가?' 로 시작하는 질문으로는 어떤 것도 해결할 수 없다. 오히려 두려움을 만들어내고, 창의성을 억누르며, 사람들 사이에 벽을 만들 뿐이다.

14. 서투른 선원이 바람을 탓한다

책임의식을 가진 사람은 누구를 탓할까? 아무도 탓하지 않는
다. 게다가 스스로를 비난하는 일도 없다.

15. 편 가르기

팀을 구성하기 위해 많은 시간과 자원을 투자하면서도 막상
중요한 사실을 잊어버릴 때가 있다. 우리 모두는 '같은 팀의 일
원' 이라는 사실 말이다. 그럼에도 불구하고 '일을 제대로 하지
않는다며' 상대팀을 헐뜯고 비난하는 경우가 적지 않다. 이런
식으로 영역을 구분하여 다툼을 일삼는 것은 조직의 생명을 고
갈시키고 아무리 노력해도 앞으로 나아갈 수 없다.

16. 심판을 이기는 법

어떤 목표를 갖든 극복해야 할 장애물은 언제나 있기 마련이
다. 당신의 힘으로는 도저히 통제할 수 없는 장애물일 수도 있
다. 이럴 때는 장애물 자체에 집착하지 말자. 심판이 아무리 불
리한 판정을 내리더라도 의연하게 성공을 향해 나아갈 수 있는
성숙함을 가지려고 노력해야 한다. 성공을 원한다면 당신의 통
제범위 밖에 있는 무언가를 불평해서는 안 된다.

17. 누가 일을 망쳤나?

중요한 건 '우리 VS 그들' 이 아니다. '왜 이렇게 많은 승객을 태웠나?' 또는 '문제의 원인이 누구에게 있는가?' 하는 것이 아니라는 얘기다. 그런 질문보다는 차라리 '상황을 호전시키기 위해 지금 당장 내가 할 수 있는 것은 무엇인가?' 를 생각하는 것이 훨씬 나은 선택이다.

18. 주인의식

문제를 '해결' 하기 위해 머리와 손과 가슴을 모두 동원하여 전념하면서도, 결코 책임을 남에게 '전가' 하지 않는 것! 이것이 바로 진정한 주인의식이다. 당신은 무언가에 이처럼 전념해본 적이 있는가?

19. 팀워크의 토대

'진정한 팀원이란 서로를 통해 나아갈 길을 찾고, 그 글에서 만족을 누릴 수 있는 사람' 이다. 팀원들이 가지고 있는 재능과 장점에 감사하자. 팀워크란 바로 여기서 비롯된다.

20. 모든 QBQ는 '나' 를 포함한다

책임의식이 있는 집단의 위력은 실로 대단하다. 관리자와 경영자는 그저 기준을 설정하여 직원들에게 알리기만 하면 된다.

개인적 책임의식으로 무장된 집단의 직원들이라면, 그 기준 속에서 자발적으로 QBQ, 즉 '무엇?' 과 '어떻게?' 로 시작하여 '나' 를 포함하는 질문이 쏟아져 나오기 때문이다.

21. 내가 변화시킬 수 있는 것은 나뿐이다

내가 변화시킬 수 있는 사람은 오직 나 자신뿐이다. 누구도 타인을 변화시킬 수는 없다. 변화란 개인의 결정에 따라 내부에서 형성되는 결과물이기 때문이다. 모든 사람들이 타인보다 스스로의 사고와 행동을 변화시키려 노력할 때 비로소 기대 이상의 성과를 만들어낼 수 있는 것이다.

22. 다른 사람이 아니라 내가 변한다

다른 사람을 변화시키겠다는 생각을 버리고 내가 변해야 한다.

23. 말 따로 행동 따로

QBQ식 사고는 말과 행동에 일관성을 유지함으로써, 내 입에서 흘러나온 나와 실제의 내가 일치하는 것이다. '언제쯤이면 사람들의 말과 행동이 일치할까? 라고 묻기 전에, 우리 스스로부터 그런 사람이 되기 위해 노력해야 한다.

24. 조직 구성원을 위한 자질 테스트

당신은 어떤 사람인가? 근무 중에는 마치 그 직장이 무척 마음
에 드는 것처럼 이야기하면서, 퇴근 후에는 완전히 돌변하여 온갖
비난을 성토하지는 않는가? 이런 사람들을 위한 답은 딱 한 가지
다. '싫으면 떠나라.' 우리가 인생의 목표를 달성하는 데 직장이
아무런 도움이 되지 않는다면 굳이 그곳에 머무를 이유가 없다.

25. 팀의 위력

개인적인 책임의식이 필요한 이유는 타인을 변화시키기 위해
서가 아니라 우리 스스로를 바꿈으로써 남다른 성과를 창출하기
위해서이다. 그리고 개인적 책임의식을 통해서만이 모두가 하나
된 힘을 발휘할 수 있다.

26. QBQ 기도문

"하느님! 부디 저에게 바꿀 수 없는 사람을 받아들일 수 있는
평정과 바꿀 수 있는 오직 한 사람을 바꿀 수 있는 용기와 이 둘
의 차이를 깨달을 수 있는 지혜를 주시옵소서!"

27. 진정한 역할 모델들이여, 일어나라!

우리의 역할이 무엇이든, 누군가는 우리의 행동을 관찰하고
흉내 낸다. 모범을 보이는 것이야말로 모든 교사들의 가장 중요

한 역할이다. 당신을 지켜보는 사람은 누구인가?

28. QBQ의 핵심은 바로 행동

"지금 당장 내가 할 수 있는 것은 무엇인가?"

무엇을 할 수 있는지 또는 무엇을 성취하거나 이룰 수 있는지 스스로에게 끊임없이 질문하지 않으면 아무것도 얻을 수 없다. 행동이 뒤따를 때 비로소 무엇이든 이루어낼 수 있는 것 아닌가?

29. 아무것도 하지 않는 것이 더욱 위험하다

어떤 직업이든 무조건적인 안정을 보장받은 자리는 어디에도 없다. 냉정하게 얘기해서 오늘 아무 행동도 하지 않는다면, 내일 당장 일자리가 없어질지도 모른다. 무언가 행동을 취하는 것이 위험스러워 보일 수도 있지만, '아무것도' 하지 않는다면 더 큰 위험을 초래할 뿐이다!

30. 홈 데포 *Home Depot*에서의 즐거운 쇼핑

모든 고객들에게 훌륭한 서비스를 제공하는 것. 이것은 위험 이나 손해를 감수할 가치가 충분히 있는 QBQ 서비스이다.

31. 리더라고 생각하는 사람이 리더이다

리더십이란 다른 어떤 것보다도 우리의 사고방식에 의해 좌우

된다. 어떤 식으로든 주변 사람들에게 영향을 미치는 존재라면 당신은 리더가 될 수 있다.

32. 리더십의 초석

서번트 리더십 *Servant Leadership* 이야말로 QBQ 방식이다. 봉사자의 마음과 겸손함을 겸비할 때 비로소 진정한 리더십을 발휘할 수 있다. 겸손은 리더십의 초석이다.

33. 리더는 문제를 해결하는 사람이 아니다

진정한 리더는 팀원들로 하여금 문제를 받아들이고, 나름대로의 해결책을 모색하며, 행동을 취하도록 유도한다. 문제를 해결해주는 식으로는 어떠한 교훈도, 배움도, 봉사도 있을 수 없다.

34. 세상의 모든 엉터리 질문들

IQ와 QBQ 중 어느 쪽을 선택할 것인가? 선택은 오직 당신에게 달려 있다. 모쪼록 현명하게 판단하길 빈다. 어떤 생각을 가지느냐에 따라 당신의 선택은 이 세상을 바꿀 수도 있다.

35. QBQ 정신

1. 피해의식, 태만, 비난에서 탈피한다.
2. 나는 오직 나만 변화시킬 수 있다.

3. 행동을 취하라!

36. 지혜 : 이미 알고 난 뒤에 배우는 것

나는 아직 완성되지 않은 상품이다.

당신도 그렇지 않은가?

37. 우리는 너무 많은 책을 산다

배움이란 세미나에 참석하고, 음악을 듣고, 책을 읽는다고 해서 저절로 얻어지는 것이 아니다. 진정한 배움이란 '알고 있는 것' 을 '행동' 으로 옮기는 과정이다. 그리고 이것이 바로 변화이다.

38. 나의 책임

각자 자신의 위치와 역할에 최선을 다해 능력을 발휘하고 상호간의 협력을 통해 위대한 결과를 이끌어내기 위해 필요한 것이 바로 QBQ이다.

39. 배움의 원동력

배움의 원동력은 반복에 있다.

About the Author

John G. Miller is the founder of QBQ, Inc., an organizational development firm dedicated to making personal accountability a core value for organizations and individuals. Together with a nationwide network of QBQ! certified consultants, Miller has brought his message to countless corporations, as well as academic, nonprofit, and government groups, including American Express, the American Cancer Society, JCPenny, Dell, Royal Bank of Canada, and Eli Lilly. He is also the author of *Flipping the Switch*. A graduate of Cornell, he lives in Denver with his wife, Karen, and their seven children.

dedicate 헌신하다 **cerified** 증명된 **countless** 셀 수 없는

About the Interpreter

정호섭, 뉴욕주립대에서 국제관계를 전공했다. 재학시절에는 조선일보 뉴욕에서 근무하기도 하였다. 뉴욕에서 여러 업체의 계약관련 업무를 담당했고 현대-기아, 신한-조흥, 엠코, LG-AD 등 많은 기업체에서 비즈니스 강의를 했다. 현재는 YBM 시사에서 비즈니스 영어를 담당하고 있다.

한언의 사명선언문

Since 3rd day of January, 1998

Our Mission
- 우리는 새로운 지식을 창출, 전파하여 전 인류가 이를 공유케 함으로써 인류문화의 발전과 행복에 이바지한다.
- 우리는 끊임없이 학습하는 조직으로서 자신과 조직의 발전을 위해 쉼없이 노력하며, 궁극적으로는 세계적 컨텐츠 그룹을 지향한다.
- 우리는 정신적, 물질적으로 최고 수준의 복지를 실현하기 위해 노력하며, 명실공히 초일류 사원들의 집합체로서 부끄럼없이 행동한다.

Our Vision 한언은 컨텐츠 기업의 선도적 성공모델이 된다.

저희 한언인들은 위와 같은 사명을 항상 가슴 속에 간직하고
좋은 책을 만들기 위해 최선을 다하고 있습니다.
독자 여러분의 아낌없는 충고와 격려를 부탁드립니다.

· 한언 가족 ·

HanEon′s Mission statement

Our Mission
- We create and broadcast new knowledge for the advancement and happiness of the whole human race.
- We do our best to improve ourselves and the organization, with the ultimate goal of striving to be the best content group in the world.
- We try to realize the highest quality of welfare system in both mental and physical ways and we behave in a manner that reflects our mission as proud members of HanEon Community.

Our Vision HanEon will be the leading Success Model of the content group.